TWAYNE'S MASTERWORK STUDIES
Robert Lecker, General Editor

THE GLASS MENAGERIE
AN AMERICAN MEMORY

THE GLASS MENAGERIE

An American Memory

DELMA E. PRESLEY

TWAYNE PUBLISHERS • BOSTON
A DIVISION OF G.K. HALL & CO.

The Glass Menagerie: An American Memory
Delma E. Presley

Twayne's Masterwork Studies No. 43

Copyright 1990 by G.K. Hall & Co.
All rights reserved.
Published by Twayne Publishers
A Division of G.K. Hall & Co.
70 Lincoln Street
Boston, Massachusetts 02111

Book production and design by Gabrielle B. McDonald
Copyediting supervised by Barbara Sutton
Typeset in 10/14 Sabon, display typeface in Galliard
by Huron Valley Graphics of Ann Arbor, Michigan

Printed on permanent/durable acid-free paper
and bound in the United States of America

Library of Congress Cataloging-in-Publication Data

Presley, Delma Eugene.
The glass menagerie : an American memory / Delma E. Presley.
p.   cm.—(Twayne's masterwork studies)
Includes bibliographical references.
Includes index.
1. Williams, Tennessee, 1911–1983. Glass menagerie.   I. Title.
II. Series.
PS3545.I5365G5365   1990
812'.54—dc20   89-38328
CIP

0-8057-8058-0 (alk. paper) 10 9 8 7 6 5 4 3 2 1
0-8057-8127-7 (pbk. alk. paper) 10 9 8 7 6 5 4 3 2 1
First published 1990

CONTENTS

NOTE ON THE REFERENCES AND ACKNOWLEDGMENTS

For page references to *The Glass Menagerie* I have used the widely available New Classics edition first published in 1949; copyright 1945 by Tennessee Williams and Edwina D. Williams; reprinted by permission of New Directions Publishing Corp. The poem "Heavenly Grass" from Tennessee Williams, *In the Winter of Cities*, © 1956 by Tennessee Williams, is reprinted by permission of New Directions Publishing Corp. The Alfred Hayes poem "In a Coffee Pot" first appeared in *Partisan Review* 1, no. 1 (1934), and is reprinted by permission.

Early in my career I was fortunate to pursue graduate studies in Emory University's interdisciplinary program in the humanities, the Graduate Institute of Liberal Arts. At that time few students and even fewer faculty there considered Tennessee Williams's works appropriate for serious study. However, the ILA challenged and encouraged me. I wish to acknowledge the influence of this stimulating academic community in my life and work. David Hesla, Thomas Altizer, Robert Wheeler, and Floyd Watkins in various ways helped me find my way as a student of American literature and culture. Later my colleagues in the classroom, Hari Singh and Hollis Cate, generously shared their insights and contributed measurably to my interpretation of *The Glass Menagerie*. The useful index reveals the expertise of my friend who prepared it: Julius Ariail, Director of Libraries at Georgia Southern College. The Georgia Southern Museum and the faculty research committee of Georgia Southern have supported my efforts. For thirty years

Note on References and Acknowledgments

Beverly has shared my work with enthusiasm and thoughtful attention to detail. In this particular project she has been assisted by our daughter Susan. Both have improved this book, and I acknowledge their assistance and encouragement.

TENNESSEE WILLIAMS
Photograph by Angus McBean, London. Courtesy of New Directions Publishing Corporation.

CHRONOLOGY:
TENNESSEE WILLIAMS'S
LIFE AND WORKS

1907   Edwina Dakin, daughter of Episcopal clergyman Walter Edwin Dakin, marries Cornelius Coffin Williams (an employee of the Cumberland Telephone Company, Spanish-American War veteran, and descendant of Thomas Lanier Williams I, the first chancellor of the Western Territory, and of John Williams, Tennessee's first senator) 2 June at her father's church in Columbus, Mississippi.

1911   Thomas Lanier Williams, named for paternal grandfather, Thomas Lanier Williams II (d. 1908), born 26 March, Palm Sunday, in Columbus, the second of three children of Edwina and Cornelius Williams—Rose Isabel (b. 1909) and Walter Dakin (b. 1919). For the next seven years Edwina, Rose, and Thomas live with the Reverend and Mrs. Dakin in rectories in Columbus; Nashville, Tennessee; Canton, Mississippi; and Clarksdale, Mississippi, receiving occasional visits from Cornelius Williams, now a traveling salesman for clothing and shoe manufacturers.

1918   Edwina, Rose, and Thomas move to St. Louis, presumably to join Cornelius Williams who had accepted a job in management with the Friedman-Shelby branch of the International Shoe Company. The three move often during the next decade in St. Louis; by the time Thomas is fifteen, he and his mother and sister have lived in over sixteen homes. During these years Thomas and Rose establish a close relationship, which influences his writing, especially *The Glass Menagerie*.

1924–1928   *Junior Life*, newspaper at Ben Blewett Junior High School, prints "A Great Tale Told at Katrina's Party," a ghost story by

Thomas Lanier Williams (October 1924), followed by a few poems in later issues. In June 1925 the school yearbook carries "Demon Smoke" about pollution in St. Louis, which earns him a $5 prize from the Citizen's Smoke Abatement League. At Soldan High he writes poems, essays, and reviews of silent movies. After transferring to University City High School, he wins a third-place prize for a letter answering the question, "Can a Good Wife Be a Good Sport?" The letter becomes his first national publication in 1927, appearing in the May issue of *Smart Set* magazine. National pulp magazine, *Weird Tales,* pays him $35 for a horror story, "The Vengeance of Nitocris" (August 1928).

1928   Makes his first trip to New York with his Grandfather Dakin, where he enjoys *Show Boat,* before departing on a church tour of Europe; he is fascinated by Gounod's *Roméo et Juliette* at the Paris Opéra.

1929   Graduates fifty-third in a class of eighty-three at University City High School; enrolls at the University of Missouri, Columbia. Reads and writes independently; his favorite authors are the dramatists Chekhov, Ibsen, and Strindberg.

1930–1931   Wins honorable mention for his first play, *Beauty Is the Word,* in a competition at the university. Becomes a member of the Alpha Tau Omega fraternity.

1932–1934   After compiling a record of Cs and Ds, with a few Bs and four Fs (all in Reserve Officers Training Corps), his father withdraws him from the university in spring 1932. He begins a job at the continental branch of the International Shoe Company warehouse, St. Louis, while continuing to write and publish poetry in various small magazines.

1935   Released from his job because of ill health in the spring of 1935. Recuperates and continues writing at his grandparents' home in Memphis. The Memphis Garden Players perform his one-act play, *Cairo! Shanghai! Bombay!*

1935–1936   Studies at Washington University, St. Louis, and continues to write poems and plays. Becomes an admirer of the poetry of Hart Crane.

1937   Fails to meet Washington University's requirements for graduation in the spring; enrolls at the University of Iowa in the fall. His first full-length plays are produced here: *The Fugitive Kind* and *Candles to the Sun.* After her nervousness and anxiety become pronounced, Rose is placed in a mental hospital. Without his knowledge, Mr. and Mrs. Williams follow a doctor's recommendation and authorize treatment of Rose with a new neurosurgical technique, the prefrontal lobotomy, leaving her calm, though institutionalized, for the rest of her life.

1938   Earns B.A. in English from the University of Iowa.

1939   First uses the name "Tennessee Williams" on a contest application form submitted with four plays called *American Blues* and wins a prize of $100. He makes a living by working in restaurants in the French Quarter in New Orleans. During travels through California, publishes "Field of Blue Children" in *Story* magazine.

1939–1940   Wins $1,000 writing fellowship from the Dramatists Guild through the Rockefeller Foundation; attends John Gassner's playwrighting seminar at the New School for Social Research; completes *Battle of Angels,* which opens to mixed reviews in Boston 30 December 1940 and runs briefly before closing.

1941–1943   Holds different jobs in Provincetown, New York, Macon, Jacksonville, and St. Louis. Begins a play based on his family, *The Gentleman Caller,* closely related to an earlier short story, "Portrait of a Girl in Glass." Accepts employment at Metro-Goldwyn-Mayer as a writer but is unable to perform according to Hollywood's guidelines. Writes drafts of several short stories and plays. Submits *The Gentleman Caller* to M-G-M, which quickly refuses to consider it.

1944   Receives $1,000 award for *Battle of Angels* from the National Institute of Arts and Letters; publishes poems in *Five Young American Poets;* completes script for *The Glass Menagerie,* similar to *The Gentleman Caller. The Glass Menagerie* opens at the Civic Theatre, Chicago, for a small audience on 26 December; supported by ticket subsidies for municipal employees and encouraged by strong reviews, the play survives; Williams assigns half of his royalties ($1,000 a week) to his mother.

1945   On 26 March (Williams's thirty-fourth birthday), *Menagerie* moves to the Playhouse Theatre in New York and receives favorable reviews when it opens on 31 March. Laurette Taylor gives a memorable performance as Amanda. In April the New York Drama Critics Circle announces that *Menagerie* wins Best American Play award on the first ballot. Other major awards follow. *Menagerie* has 561 performances. In September *You Touched Me!* a comedy coauthored with Donald Windham, opens to mixed reviews at New York's Booth Theatre and has 100 performances.

1946   *Menagerie* with its Broadway cast is chosen for the Roosevelt Birthday Celebration command performance at the National Theatre, Washington, D.C., 27 January. Publishes *27 Wagons Full of Cotton and Other Plays*. Completes manuscript for *Ten Blocks on the Camino Real*. Moves to Nantucket Island during the summer and befriends Carson McCullers, who stays with him while she works on her play, *The Member of the Wedding*. They remain friends until her death in 1967.

1947   *A Streetcar Named Desire*, formerly *Poker Night*, opens 3 December and is applauded for a half-hour on opening night; wins Pulitzer Prize, New York Drama Critics Circle Award, and Donaldson Award and has 855 performances.

1948   *Menagerie* opens 28 July at the Savoy Theatre, London, directed by John Gielgud and starring Helen Hayes. *Summer and Smoke* opens 6 October and runs for 100 performances after receiving several negative reviews. Publishes *American Blues: Five Short Plays* and *One Arm and Other Stories*.

1949   Travels in Italy and Europe. Visits London to discuss April opening of *Streetcar* with director Laurence Olivier. Moves to a new home in Key West, joined by his grandfather, the Reverend Dakin.

1950   Warner Brothers releases film of *Menagerie*, and Williams disapproves of the movie's "happy ending." Publishes the novel *The Roman Spring of Mrs. Stone* and writes introduction to Carson McCullers's novel *Reflections in a Golden Eye*.

1951   On 3 February *The Rose Tattoo* begins a run of 300 performances during a season that includes *South Pacific, Darkness at Noon, Guys and Dolls, Call Me Madam*, and *Bell, Book and Candle*. Wins the Tony award for the best play. Publishes *I Rise in Flame, Cried the Phoenix*, a play concerning the death of D. H. Lawrence.

1952   In April *Summer and Smoke* begins a successful year-long Broadway revival. Sells rights to this play and *The Rose Tattoo* to Paramount for $100,000 each. On 28 May is elected as lifetime member of the National Institute of Arts and Letters.

1953   The antifascist play, *Camino Real* opens 19 March and receives largely negative reviews, which Williams relates to the politically repressive atmosphere encouraged by Senator Joseph McCarthy. Closes after sixty performances.

1954   Publishes *Hard Candy: A Book of Stories* and continues to write at his home in Key West, Florida.

Chronology: Tennessee Williams's Life and Works

1955   Longtime companion Grandfather Dakin dies 14 February at the age of ninety-seven, leaving Williams half of his estate of $200. *Cat on a Hot Tin Roof* opens to enthusiastic reviews 24 March, beginning a run of 694 performances. Wins his third New York Drama Critics Circle Award and second Pulitzer Prize.

1956   Comic film *Baby Doll* premieres 18 December; Francis Cardinal Spellman suggests it will "contribute to corruption in America," and *Time* magazine notes it is "possibly the dirtiest American-made motion picture." Publishes a book of poems, *In The Winter of Cities*.

1957   *Orpheus Descending* opens 21 March and closes after sixty-eight performances. On 27 March his father dies in Knoxville, Tennessee, at the age of seventy-seven. Begins a year of intense psychotherapy in New York and spends time with sister, Rose, who lives at a residence hospital nearby.

1958   *Suddenly Last Summer* and *Something Unspoken* open on 7 January and run for 216 performances under the title *Garden District*. Kraft Television Theatre on 16 April produces "Moony's Kid Don't Cry," "The Last of My Solid Gold Watches," and "This Property Is Condemned," all written before 1944.

1959   *Sweet Bird of Youth* opens 10 March. Critics and audiences notice the playwright's treatment of drug addiction, alcoholism, prostitution, venereal disease, and racism. Sells movie rights for $400,000; his royalties during the ninety-five stage performances are $1,500 daily.

1960   *Period of Adjustment,* a domestic comedy, receives good reviews when it opens 10 November. He regularly takes prescription drugs to relieve nervousness and depression.

1961   *The Night of the Iguana* opens 28 December. Wins New York Drama Critics Circle Award and London Critics' Poll for Best New Foreign Play.

1962   Appears on the cover of *Time* Magazine, and an essay inside calls him "a consummate master of theater." Brief version of *The Milk Train Doesn't Stop Here Anymore* opens at Festival of the Two Worlds, Spoleto, Italy.

1963   *Milk Train* opens 16 January and receives mixed reviews. Williams resumes intense psychotherapy and continues use of alcohol and drugs.

1964   M-G-M releases the popular film production of *The Night of the Iguana,* the twelfth film to have been produced from Williams's plays. Film rights for his plays now account for several million dollars in his bank account. His short story "Grand," a tribute to his grandmother Dakin, appears in a limited edition by House of Books, Ltd., in December.

1965   *Menagerie* appears in a twentieth-anniversary production at the Brooks Atkinson Theatre 4 May.

1966   *Slapstick Tragedy* (*The Mutilated* and *The Gnadiges Fraulein*) opens 22 February and closes at the end of one week. CBS-TV produces *Menagerie* 8 December. Williams publishes *The Knightly Quest: A Novella and Four Short Stories.*

1967   *The Two-Character Play* plays briefly at the Hampstead Theatre Club, London, 27 November.

1968   *The Seven Descents of Myrtle,* starring Estelle Parsons and Harry Guardino, receives poor reviews after opening 27 March and closes after twenty-nine performances.

1969   In January converts to Catholicism and travels to Rome to meet with church officials but later resumes his previous style of living. *In the Bar of a Tokyo Hotel* opens for a run of twenty-five performances 11 May. Receives the gold medal from the National Institute of Arts and Letters on 21 May "in recognition of his dramatic works, which reveal a poetic imagination and a gift for characterization that are rare in the contemporary theatre." Spends the fall in a hospital in St. Louis and withdraws from dependence on drugs and alcohol.

1970   Travels for three months in Asia after the publication of *Dragon Country: A Book of Plays.*

1971   Revised version of *The Two-Character Play* opens in Chicago under the title *Out Cry.* Williams acknowledges the play's subject is his relationship to his sister, Rose. Resumes use of alcohol and drugs.

1972   *Small Craft Warnings* opens off-Broadway 2 April, his last effort to receive favorable reviews, and runs for 194 performances. Purdue University awards him an honorary doctorate.

1973   Revised *Out Cry* runs for ten performances in New York. Interviews for radio, television, and magazines reveal details of private life, especially the interview in the April issue of *Playboy* magazine. ABC-TV produces *Menagerie* 16 December and wins an Emmy award.

Chronology: Tennessee Williams's Life and Works

1974   Travels throughout the United States, visiting his sister, Rose, at her residence-hospital in New York; speaks often of the role of religion in his life, and begins writing three new plays. Publishes *Eight Mortal Ladies Possessed: A Book of Stories*.

1975   *The Red Devil Battery Sign* opens in Boston 18 June and runs for seventeen performances. Publishes the novel *Moise and the World of Reason* and his autobiography, *Memoirs*. *Menagerie* is revived for a limited engagement 18 December in New York.

1976   *This Is (an Entertainment)* opens for a short run in San Francisco. He suffers periods of anxiety and disorientation induced by drugs and alcohol.

1977   A play based on his youth, *Vieux Carré*, opens and closes after five performances. Returns to Key West and erects a household shrine to his sister, Rose, including photos of her and St. Jude, patron of hopeless cases.

1978   Spoleto Festival in Charleston, South Carolina, features *Creve Coeur* (translated "heartbreak"), a play set in St. Louis in the 1930s, as well as an exhibition of his paintings. Publishes *Where I Live: Selected Essays*. Leases apartment in New York, and Rose spends the Christmas holidays with him.

1979   *A Lovely Sunday for Creve Coeur* opens 21 January and runs for thirty-six performances. Purchases second home in Key West and arranges for Rose and an attendent to move there; Rose returns to her hospital after one year. He receives membership in the Theatre Hall of Fame. Receives the Kennedy Honors Award.

1980   Based on the life of F. Scott Fitzgerald and wife, Zelda, *Clothes for a Summer Hotel* opens and closes after fourteen performances. Williams remarks that the character Zelda is patterned after his sister, Rose. Mother, Edwina, dies 1 June. Within a week of the funeral, President Jimmy Carter awards him the Medal of Freedom at a White House ceremony and Williams lauds the president's "humanitarianism." *Menagerie* is revived in New York 5 November.

1981   *A House Not Meant to Stand* opens 1 April and runs briefly in Chicago, featuring a character, Cornelius, the name of Williams's father.

1982   *Something Cloudy, Something Clear*, an autobiographical play about Williams's earlier years, opens 7 February. His last performed play, *A House Not Meant to Stand*, revised, opens for a month's engagement in Chicago; reviews are largely favorable. He receives an honorary doctorate from Harvard University.

1983   Dies in his room at the Elysee Hotel, New York, 25 February. An autopsy reveals that he had choked on a small medicine bottle cap. He is buried in St. Louis between his mother and a grave reserved for his sister, Rose; his will generously provides for her care and comfort as long as she lives. On 1 December at New York's Eugene O'Neill Theatre, *Menagerie* is revived again, incorporating for the first time on Broadway many of Williams's screen projections noted in the original reading text.

CHAPTER 1

Historical Context

With a characteristic touch of irony Tom Wingfield begins *The Glass Menagerie* by remembering the 1930s as a "quaint period." His approach prepares the audience for his poignant memory. The stage itself is "quaint." It contains just enough in the way of furnishings—the Victrola, the cabinet of glass figures, the typewriter—to suggest that those who live here somehow do not quite belong in this apartment, whose entrance from a narrow alley is an ugly fire escape. As Tom's opening monologue makes clear, however, twentieth-century America itself was experiencing a surprising turn of events. He looks back on his family's experience and realizes that they belong to a larger drama whose cast includes millions of Americans.

If the Great Depression was anything, it was unexpected. Americans had been told the thirties would be a decade of peace and prosperity. In his final message to Congress on 4 December 1928, President Calvin Coolidge said that citizens should "regard the present with satisfaction and anticipate the future with optimism." Coolidge was succeeded by Herbert Hoover who predicted that poverty soon would be virtually nonexistent. Even after the Wall Street crash of 24 and 29 October 1929, government officials continued to speak optimistically about the future. According to Andrew Mellon, secretary of the treasury, the economic situation was not "menacing"; certainly nothing "warrants pessimism," he concluded.

As Tom bittersweetly recalls, Americans—especially those who lived in the cities that depended on offices and plants to provide jobs—learned some hard lessons. In Detroit nearly 130,000 people received salaries from the Ford Motor Company in early 1929. By August 1931 fewer than 40,000 were on the payroll. The trend nationwide was not encouraging. Between 1929 and 1932 the national income fell from $81 billion to $41 billion. Wages declined by 60 percent. Tom speaks of "disturbances of labor, sometimes pretty violent, in otherwise peaceful cities such as Chicago, Cleveland, Saint Louis." And for rural America in 1933 there was the "dustbowl blues," as go the lyrics of a popular song by Woody Guthrie. Wind storms ravaged farmlands in the West; the unclouded skies that followed were darkened by waves of grasshoppers that destroyed any crops the winds had spared. By the mid-thirties over 350,000 farmers had left their fields and were moving in search of work. John Steinbeck's *Grapes of Wrath* starkly chronicles the wandering and starving masses, especially Oklahoma's displaced farmers.

Americans were learning some new lessons left out of their school books. Speaking as a poet, Tom explains that Americans' "eyes had failed them, or they had failed their eyes, and so they were having their fingers pressed forcibly down on the fiery Braille alphabet of a dissolving economy." Amanda Wingfield speaks for a generation when she tells Jim O'Connor: "I wasn't prepared for what the future brought me." This point of view permeates a poem by Alfred Hayes that appeared in 1934. Hayes depicts the dejection of the unemployed middle class. Among them were educated men and women who had attempted to play by the rules throughout their lives, only to discover that the guidelines of their elders were of little help:

> I brood upon myself, I rot
> Night after night in this cheap coffee pot.
> I am twenty-two I shave each day

Historical Context

> I was educated at a public school
> They taught me what to read and what to say
> The nobility of man my country's pride
> How Nathan Hale died
> And Grant took Richmond.
> Was it on a summer or a winter's day?
> Was it Sherman burned the Southland to the sea?
> The men the names the dates have worn away
> The classes words the books commencement prize
> Here bitter with myself I sit
> Holding the ashes of their prompted lies.[1]

More succinct is Tom's opening monologue: "America was matriculating in a school for the blind." The confusion not only prevailed on the home front. As a nation among nations, the United States seemed out of step. Despite newspaper headlines about the dramatic political changes sweeping Europe, citizens were unmoved; among them surely were those patrons who flocked to the Paradise Dance Hall across the alley from the Wingfields' apartment, searching for diversions as they danced to the tune "All the World Is Waiting for the Sunrise." In fact, as Tom reminds the audience, "All the world was waiting for bombardments!"

Germany in the early 1930s witnessed the death of the German Republic and the birth of the Third Reich, headed by the dictator Adolf Hitler. In Italy the scenario was similar; the dictator there was Benito Mussolini. Even in America some influential leaders believed that only a dictator like Governor Huey Long of Louisiana could lead the country out of the economic depression. The journalist William Randolph Hearst did not object to the notion, explaining that a person who is called a fascist is usually nothing more than a "loyal citizen who stands for Americanism."

Many intellectuals and writers throughout the world were deeply interested in world politics. The struggle against fascism in Spain inspired Stephen Vincent Benet, Theodore Dreiser, Arthur Koestler, André Malraux, Edna St. Vincent Millay, Stephen Spender, and many others who wrote and spoke in behalf of the Loyalists who often lost their lives opposing the dictatorship. (*The Glass Menagerie* contains several references to the Spanish struggle.) Ernest Hemingway strongly supported efforts of the Spanish to overthrow the fascist regime. By 1937 he personally had raised $40,000 to provide ambulances and medicine for the Loyalist resistance. In Hemingway's words, "Fascism is a lie told by bullies."

The Glass Menagerie reflects other historical and social realities of the 1930s and 1940s. A child of the South, Williams was deeply influenced by the land in which his roots ran deep. The playwright was the third member of his family to bear the name Thomas Lanier Williams. The first was chancellor of the Western Territory (Tennessee); another ancestor was the state's first senator. But Williams's family history also includes episodes of profligate behavior: his paternal grandfather, Thomas Lanier Williams II, was an unsuccessful politician who lost the family fortune while repeatedly and vainly seeking the governorship of Tennessee. A bright feature of the family lineage is the poet Sidney Lanier. At times Williams's writings remind one of the poet of nineteenth-century Georgia who wrote musical poems such as "The Song of the Chattahoochee" and "Marshes of Glynn." Williams published two volumes of poems, and critics often have remarked that the language of his better plays is the language of poetry.

If Williams's characters' voices resound with the music of southern speech, their patterns of thought also reflect regional characteristics that some critics call the myth of the South. Although Amanda and her children live in a small apartment in a crowded midwestern city, she constantly speaks of her girlhood in Mississippi, a land of chivalry and romance. Margaret Mitchell's best-selling novel, *Gone with the Wind* (1936), had made the South a part of the national consciousness, and Amanda mentions the novel in one of her telephone conversations. She refers to her daughter as "sister" and speaks about her past. She also reveals another characteristic of many southerners: the influence of religion. The daughter of an Episcopal clergyman, Amanda insists on beginning meals with a traditional blessing. She weaves familiar biblical quotations ("Possess your soul in patience!") into her conversation, and she vigorously upholds traditional morality when she criticizes Tom's choice of reading material, as well as his drinking, smoking, and carousing.

Williams achieved success a few years too late to be considered a part of the so-called southern renaissance, a movement that profoundly influenced twentieth-century literature. At Vanderbilt University in the 1920s, a group of writers known as the Agrarians had sought to focus national attention on the region's cultural and literary heritage, a birthright they considered extremely valuable though often misunderstood. The Agrarians chief members were Allen Tate, John Crowe Ransom, Robert Penn Warren, and Donald Davidson. Two well-known authors of this period, William Faulkner and Thomas Wolfe, wrote award-winning novels about the impact of the past on the lives of southerners. Although *The Glass Menagerie* appeared in the mid-1940s, it focuses on a theme common to other southern writers of this period: the family unit. In this regard the play reminds one of William Faulkner's probing novels, such as *The Sound and the Fury,* that explore the breakdown of historic families during a time of social and cultural change.

The playwright's imaginary world lies in the heart of the Mississippi Delta whose small towns have colorful names like Glorious Hill and Blue Mountain. In *The Glass Menagerie,* as in most of his other work, Williams reveals that his heart belongs to the South. He chose the nickname *Tennessee* because he identified with his pioneer ancestors. A number of his characters reveal his fondness for southern traditions. Yet although Williams could be nostalgic, he also looked upon his South with a critical eye. He would not allow his plays to be performed in segregated theaters at least a decade before Congress enacted civil rights legislation. The region's past means much more than the magnolias, mint juleps, cotillion dances, and gentlemen callers fondly recalled by Amanda Wingfield. While Amanda recalls experiencing many moments of elegance as a belle, she also acknowledges that the past has left her empty-handed as she attempts to cope with the present.

The 1930s shocked not only Amanda but many other Americans who had moved from small-town America to bustling urban areas like

St. Louis, the nation's fourth largest city at the time. It was not only the impersonal nature of city life that bothered the Amandas of this time. They also were disillusioned by shifting attitudes toward marriage, the family, and sex. Sigmund Freud's psychological writings had focused the world's attention on subjects previously undiscussed. The British author D. H. Lawrence suggested humans should acknowledge that, like animals, they are driven by natural instincts that motivate both impulse and action. Many Americans in the 1930s, however, would have agreed with Amanda, who believed that cultivated people should avoid the "common and vulgar."

Like the character Tom, Thomas Lanier Williams embraced the notion that instinct is a compelling motivation for human behavior. In a larger sense, the playwright accepted the psychological view of humanity. Williams especially was fond of the poetry of Hart Crane and the prose of D. H. Lawrence, although in *The Glass Menagerie* their influence is not as obvious as in other plays. The themes of many of his later plays can be traced to both authors, as well as to the European dramatists of the nineteenth and early twentieth centuries. Even so, Williams hardly regarded himself as an intellectual force among twentieth-century dramatists. America's first great playwright, Eugene O'Neill, certainly probed his characters' psychological motivations with greater intensity.

Williams essentially wanted to write memorable dramas that hold the attention of the audience. He was widely read and knowledgeable about cultural and international affairs. But first and foremost he was a dramatist of the modern stage. He belonged to the first generation of Americans born in the twentieth century. He attended three very good midwestern universities—The University of Missouri, Washington University, and the University of Iowa—and graduated from the last with a major in English. Williams also studied playwrighting with a master of the modern theater, John Gassner, at the New School of Social Research in New York.

Something motivated Williams more profoundly than the intellectual currents of the 1930s and 1940s. He said in his production notes to *The Glass Menagerie* that he wanted to create unique and memorable dramas because he believed America needed a new kind of theater of "a mobile, plastic quality" (xii). As a young man Williams had spent thousands of hours in movie houses watching silent films with titles and captions, productions accompanied by a live piano or a small orchestra. Since movies were dramas produced on film for an audience, Williams reasoned that he could write dramas for the stage that benefited from techniques used by the makers of movies. This is why his production notes discuss how and when the screen projections, lighting, and music would be employed. The playwright who admired the works of Anton Chekhov, Henrik Ibsen, and August Strindberg wanted to make his own mark in the history of the drama. He did just that.

Shortly after Williams died in 1983, critics began to assess his career. They were faced with an impressive body of work: sixty-three produced or published plays, four books of short stories, two volumes of poetry, two novels, a collection of essays, a volume of letters, and his *Memoirs*. Of the fifteen films adapted from his works, he wrote or coauthored seven of them. For good reason some regard him as the only true writer in the history of American theater. Four of his plays received New York Critics Circle awards and two the coveted Pulitzer Prize. During his lifetime many agreed that he was the only American dramatist of stature after Eugene O'Neill. Upon his death more than one wrote that he was the best in the history of American theater.

CHAPTER 2

The Importance of the Work

Let us be honest. We do not go to the theater because we are interested in identifying a play's plot and theme or the interrelationship of characters onstage. The theater seats have no fold-out desk tops, and the audience is not encouraged to take notes. The playbill contains nothing resembling an exam. The truth of the matter is that we go to the theater to be entertained.

Certainly there is a great deal of entertainment in *The Glass Menagerie*. When it first was produced in Chicago on 26 December 1944, the small audience was captivated by the character Amanda as portrayed by Laurette Taylor, an older actress whose career had been in eclipse for two decades. The review that appeared in the *Chicago Tribune* the following day carried this headline: "Fragile Drama Holds Theater in Tight Spell." These words still speak for most who experience this play for the first time. The tense encounters and tender moments involving a mother, her two children, and a visitor are captivating. But there is more, and the play's first critic realized this fact. Chicago's Civic Theatre had introduced the author of "a tough little play that knows people and how they tick."[1]

The pleasure of experiencing a good play comes immediately. We are touched or infuriated, bored or intrigued, tickled or saddened, or perhaps we experience all of these feelings. But sometimes when we leave the darkened room and adjust our eyes to the light of the everyday world outside, we ask why we like or dislike what we have seen. It is then that we begin to relate the spectacle onstage to what we have learned about life, to knowledge we have gained inside and outside the classroom. Most dramas that reach the level of professional production provide audiences with some entertainment. *The Glass Menagerie* goes beyond the essentials. Long after the lights have been dimmed in the small Wingfield apartment, we remember those characters who resemble people we have known, perhaps who resemble even ourselves.

This is the difference, then, between enjoying an entertaining play and experiencing a masterwork; both events provide pleasure immediately, but one mark of greatness in a play is its ability to give audiences insight long after they have left the theater. Authors of great dramas grasp audiences in the most vulnerable place—the imagination—and lead them as far as they care to go down the road toward self-discovery, toward a clearer understanding of "people and how they tick." As he wrote in the production notes, Williams's goal was to present nothing less than "truth, life, or reality."

The Glass Menagerie is evidence that he achieved his goal. It also is evidence of his larger contribution to the literature of modern drama. He said his approach to reality could be described as a kind of "expressionism." Before writing this play, Williams had been searching for a way to explore life's subtle motivations and fragile emotions. He knew that expressionist painters often keenly portrayed hidden qualities of human subjects; he especially was impressed with their imaginative use of light and shadow. Before the production of his first successful play, with few exceptions the American stage had been realistic and conventional. While he was influenced both by artists and by other playwrights, Williams should be given credit for being at the forefront of a major new direction in modern drama. His work contrasts sharply with more conventional and realistic plays.

In his production notes, Williams encourages directors of the play to take "a lot of poetic license" with lighting, music, transparent screens, and projections of images. Directors of this and subsequent plays were given far more freedom than playwrights previously had permitted. Actors and actresses became means for directors to achieve their ends while also serving the intention of the playwright. The founder of the Actors Studio, Elia Kazan, and his successor, Lee Strasberg, based much of their theory on concepts set forth by Williams. Both established reputations as innovative directors, and their approach can be seen in many plays and films produced after World War II. Some of their best students launched acting careers by playing roles in Williams's plays; among them were Marlon Brando, Ben Gazzara, Paul Newman, Eli Wallach, Maureen Stapleton, Burl Ives, Barbara Bel Geddes, Geraldine Page, and Karl Malden.

Once the herald of a new kind of theater, *The Glass Menagerie* now has become one of the world's most widely performed and anthologized plays. Unquestionably it is a modern classic. Interpreters of the drama often attribute its success primarily to the author's mastery of form and characterization, overlooking the literary content. Just as Shakespeare's achievement cannot be measured by his mastery of theatrical technique alone, so it is with Williams. From a broader perspective, considering it as both a performance and a piece of literature, this work achieves its strength from the playwright's skillful combination of three fundamentals of drama: technique, setting, and theme.

First, this "memory play," as the author preferred to classify it, effectively uses lighting, music, screens, and other devices to reveal how past events can forcefully affect the present. Second, set in a bleak period of American history, it provides insight into the ways different members of a family cope with forces of change. Finally the play explores a universal conflict between the urge toward self-fulfillment and the love of family, a conflict that often arises when an individual seeks independence. There are other achievements in his first long-running play, of course, but these three are fundamental.

Several years after *The Glass Menagerie* opened and had made the author's colorful name a familiar part of the cultural vocabulary, Tennessee Williams wrote an essay that often appears as a preface to the play. It is entitled "The Catastrophe of Success." He writes with mixed emotions about being "snatched out of virtual oblivion and thrust into sudden prominence." He found that the round of parties and superficial conversation provoked him to yawn and left him uneasy. To become a celebrity had not been his driving force. What he took most seriously was his belief that he could not depict truth upon the stage if he were not, first, true to himself. Good drama, surely even a good life, he explains, involves an "obsessive interest in human affairs, plus a certain amount of compassion and moral conviction."[2] Granted, the story of his career makes clear that the playwright never found it easy to keep faith with the high standards he early espoused. Throughout his life he found himself constantly struggling to write what he preferred to call "the truth." For him truth was not the result of philosophical inquiry or analytical thought. He approached the subject as an artist and explained that one who is true to one's art first must be true to oneself. His dictum is as follows: "The only somebody worth being is the solitary and unseen you that existed from your first breath" ("The Catastrophe of Success," an introduction to *The Glass Menagerie* [xviii]).

Between 1944 and 1983 the author of those words never stopped struggling, even as he experienced again and again the "catastrophe of success." Beneath it all, however, beneath the surface of America's most successful and innovative dramatist, was the soft-spoken southerner whose best and most truthful work concerns a young man named Tom who looks into his past for the truth about his "solitary and unseen" self. Perhaps this play continues to touch those who experience it because we recognize in Tom's past so much that is our own.

CHAPTER 3

Critical Reception

A new play by a struggling playwright at Chicago's Civic Theatre opened the night after Christmas 1944. The audience was small, and they certainly would have been surprised had anyone told them they were witnessing the birth of a classic of the modern stage. Impassively they watched the characters make their way through the script virtually for the first time. Finally the cast of four bowed to polite and scattered applause. Such was opening night for *The Glass Menagerie*.

The weary author and cast were disappointed but not completely surprised. Rehearsals had not gone well. Williams blamed the location for some of his problems. After the actor Eddie Dowling had requested a last-minute rewrite of some of Tom Wingfield's monologue, Williams replied: "Mr. Dowling, art is experience remembered in tranquility. And I find no tranquility in Chicago." In truth the cast and crew needed an additional week for rehearsals. As late as Christmas eve Williams had not written some of the dialogue in its final form, and the actors were having trouble memorizing their lines. Furthermore the gifted actress chosen to portray Amanda, Laurette Taylor, frustrated Williams; he complained that her characterization was somewhere between "Gone with the Wind" and "the Aunt Jemima Pancake

Hour." Williams confided to a friend that the director, Margo Jones, was like "a scoutmaster leading a wayward and desperate troop to their doom."

On the afternoon of 27 December, the producers decided to close the play and prepared a notice. They were disheartened by the response of those in the half-empty house on opening night. They also were concerned that, only a few hours before the next performance, box office receipts amounted to a mere $400. They delayed posting the "Closed" sign, however, because they read reviews which had appeared earlier that morning.

"The play has the courage of true poetry couched in colloquial prose," wrote the reviewer Ashton Stevens in the *Chicago Herald American*. Claudia Cassidy, writing for the *Chicago Daily Tribune*, acknowledged that "the play is still fluid with change, but it is vividly written, and in the main superbly acted." The playwright "has been unbelievably lucky," Cassidy wrote, noting that Eddie Dowling had fought to keep the production alive, in addition to playing the role of Tom. She praised the lighting director, Joe Mielziner, "who devoted his first time out of the army service to lighting it magnificently." Subject for special praise was Laurette Taylor "who chose it for her return to the stage. [Williams] found other people, too, but ah, that Laurette Taylor." It was as though the audience and critics had witnessed different plays.[1]

Many great literary works have attracted audiences and achieved acclaim in spite of the critics. *The Glass Menagerie,* on the other hand, is a rarity. Favorable reviews and encouragement by drama critics saved the play from an early demise. The manager of the Civic Theatre urged the mayor of Chicago to authorize a 50 percent ticket subsidy for city employees. Miss Taylor refined the role of Amanda as the play struggled into the early weeks of January 1945. Although box office sales remained flat, the producers decided to keep the play open, mainly because both Ashton and Cassidy returned to the theater often and wrote about the play several times each week. By late January the theater began to post sold-out notices before each performance, and Williams's agent, Audrey Wood, started negotiating with a New York theater. On 31 March, the evening before Easter, the play opened at

New York's Playhouse Theatre. Unlike those early audiences in Chicago, this one responded with enthusiasm. The appreciative opening-night crowd applauded the cast onstage for twenty-five successive bows.

With remarkable unanimity New York's critics regarded the play as a significant event, even in a season that already had witnessed three hits: *Harvey, I Remember Mama,* and *A Bell for Adano.* The conservative *Catholic World* carried a favorable review and noted that the Legion of Decency had placed the play on the "white list" as Class A—suitable for all Catholics. Reviews of the play in *Life, Time,* and *Newsweek* attributed much of its impact to the moving portrayal of Amanda by Laurette Taylor. Only George Jean Nathan found reason to object; he wrote that it was "less a play than a palette of sub-Chekhovian pastels brushed up into a charming resemblance of one." Nevertheless, as Nathan acknowledged, the drama offers "by long odds the most imaginative evening that the stage has offered in this season."[2]

A number of reviewers immediately suggested that the play is a first-rate contribution to the modern stage. "This play is an event of the first importance," Burton Rascoe concluded in his review for the *New York World-Telegram.* In the *New York Sun,* Ward Morehouse wrote of *The Glass Menagerie* as "fragile and poignant . . . a vivid, eerie and curiously enchanting play." The theater critic Stark Young was baffled by the strong performance of Miss Taylor and agreed that the author had incorporated "free and true" characters: "I recognize them inch by inch, and I should know, for I come from the same part of the country . . . that Mr. Williams does."[3]

The first of many prizes awarded to *The Glass Menagerie* came two weeks after its New York opening: the New York Drama Critics Circle Award for the best American play of the 1944–45 season. The choice, made on the first ballot, was overwhelming. The National Theatre honored Williams and his Broadway cast by staging a command performance on 27 January 1946, the occasion of the Roosevelt birthday celebration. That Williams had achieved a place in modern theater was further acknowledged in 1948 when Sir John Gielgud directed Helen Hayes in the role of Amanda at London's Savoy Theatre. By 1952 *A Streetcar Named Desire* had further established his reputation, and he was elected to lifetime membership in the National Institute of Arts and Letters. In 1955, after a successful opening of *Cat on a Hot Tin Roof,* he won his third New York Drama Critics Circle Award and his second Pulitzer Prize.

A critical consensus about the role of *The Glass Menagerie* in the larger body of Williams's work emerged in the mid-1950s. After seeing a popular revival of the play in 1956, starring Helen Hayes, John Chapman wrote in the *New York Daily News* that it was "Tennessee Willliams's finest play"; Chapman called attention to its "affectionate, compassionate, and poetic" qualities. Brooks Atkinson agreed in his review in the *New York Times:* "Although Mr. Williams has written some overwhelming dramas since 1945, he has not written anything so delicate and perceptive." On the play's twentieth-anniversary revival in 1965, critics confirmed the consensus of the previous decade. Walter Kerr wrote in the *New York Herald Tribune* that the play is "firm as a rock today," because the playwright is "ruthlessly fair." Ten years later the play ran on Broadway with Maureen Stapleton as Amanda, and Clive Barnes reminded readers of the *Times* that *The Glass Menagerie* is more than a successful play; when first produced some thirty years earlier, it meant "a new dawn for the American theatre."[4]

The Eugene O'Neill Theatre provided the setting for a memorable production starring Jessica Tandy in December 1983, a posthumous tribute to the playwright. It was the theatrical world's acknowledgment that Williams's first successful drama had become his legacy to the modern theater.

Until his death the prolific Williams continued to write plays that attracted audiences and attention in the daily press; critics and reviewers assumed either that he had a new play in the works or that he was anticipating a revival of an earlier success. Meanwhile *The Glass Menagerie* was becoming a classic. College and university theaters produced it more often than any other play during the 1950s and 1960s. Like Shakespeare's complex hero Hamlet, Williams's Amanda became the ultimate challenge for actresses in theatrical companies—from the little theaters of small-town America to Broadway's finest. Indeed some of the most heralded actresses of the twentieth-century stage have portrayed Amanda, including Julie Haydon, Helen Hayes, Katharine Hepburn, Gertrude Lawrence, Ruth Nelson, Maureen Stapleton, Jessica Tandy, and Joanne Woodward. Laurette Taylor rendered the benchmark performance as the original Amanda.

In the 1960s the play began to appear in a few anthologies of literature, encouraging scholars to publish interpretations of Williams's works. Students of literature thus began to consider the literary significance of Tennessee Williams's plays. Yet Williams's body of work, including his first successful drama, has not been analyzed intensively by critics and interpreters in academe. Few well-known academic critics have written about his plays. Anthologies of American and southern literature sometimes fail to mention his works. While numerous critical essays and articles and several books were published between 1955 and 1985, most focus on the playwright's contribution to dramatic technique. There also has been a great deal of attention to the grotesque subject matter of many of his plays. In 1986 W. Kenneth Holditch published an appreciative essay that focuses on Williams's contemporary literary reputation. He concludes that those who write about the theater—staging, dramatic technique, characterization— take Williams seriously primarily because he so thoroughly mastered dramatic technique. Those who discuss the plays as literature, on the other hand, are few in number. Holditch concludes:

> Unfortunately, literary scholars have to a surprising extent ignored the writings of Williams. The reason for this neglect, other than the fact of his central works' overlapping of the two disciplines, is not clear. Critics in the field of drama, on the other hand, have concentrated on mechanical aspects of production and technical elements of plays rather than on plot, character, and the component parts of Williams's often very poetic language.[5]

According to Richard Vowles, the neglect of Williams's work by critics—even after he had been applauded by literary colleagues of stature—may suggest that critics typically refuse to consider seriously works that prove popular at the box office.

> In spite of his undeniable stature at home and abroad, Tennessee Williams has met with slight critical approbation. If not actively contemptuous, the little magazines had been cold. The acceptance of the ephemeral press, admittedly a mixed dish, has been succeeded by querulous denial, irritability, and more frequently, silence from literary quarters. The reasons are not far to seek.
>
> Mr. Williams has been too successful and success on Broadway has come to be equated with the slick masquerading of the shoddy. Granted that Eugene O'Neill too has had his recent Broadway successes, but we may flatter ourselves that these amount to belated recognition of a high seriousness wanted in Tennessee Williams.[6]

A reason for the low level of interest in Williams among academic critics probably reflects not so much on his writing as on the state of dramatic literature in America. Make a list of great American plays, and compare it with an English or a French list. Better still, review those American authors who have written enduring and influential poetry and prose. Their names are familiar: the poets Walt Whitman, Emily Dickinson, T. S. Eliot, William Carlos Williams, Hart Crane, Robert Frost, Wallace Stevens, Robert Penn Warren; the novelists Nathaniel Hawthorne, Herman Melville, Mark Twain, Henry James, Willa Cather, Stephen Crane, Theodore Dreiser, F. Scott Fitzgerald, Ernest Hemingway, William Faulkner, Walker Percy, and Flannery O'Connor, to name a few. These writers have given the world works of the imagination whose roots go deep into literary tradition and whose influence casts a large shadow. One who is asked to compose a comparable list of American playwrights of equal depth and breadth is given to pause and beg for more time.

Harold Bloom, Sterling Professor of Humanities at Yale, has published a number of volumes of literary criticism. In his introduction to a collection of essays about Williams published in 1987, Bloom places the literary reputation of Williams in the larger perspective of American dramatic literature. He finds works of five playwrights to be among those "dramatic works that matter most": Eugene O'Neill, Thornton Wilder, Arthur Miller, Edward Albee, and Tennessee Williams. Of the lot Williams was most prolific and "successful," Bloom maintains. More important is the matter of "significance." Among those mentioned, Bloom concludes that the "most literary . . . and clearly I mean 'literary' in a precisely descriptive sense, neither pejorative nor eulogistic, was Tennessee Williams." Often Williams acknowledged that he was influenced deeply by the dramatists Chekhov and Ibsen. D. H. Lawrence also played a role in his development as an author, but the most significant literary influence was the poet Hart Crane. Bloom suggests that Williams, like Crane, created an identity for himself as an artist. Unlike Crane who committed suicide at the age of thirty-two, Williams "outlived his own vision." Both Williams and his art gradually declined from 1953 to 1983, Bloom maintains. His early works especially reveal his true genius.[7]

Literary critics often have debated whether Williams is a "minor" or "major" (or "minor-major") author; not all agree with Bloom's high assessment. Drama critics and reviewers for newspapers and magazines have been more consistent, however. Since his death, few have disputed the judgment that the playwright stands securely as a major figure in the history of the drama. Some argue that he stands second to O'Neill. Others maintain he is second to none.

Evaluation of the place of Williams is only one aspect of the critic's task, and a rather limited one at that. By far the most significant issue is the nature of Williams's achievement. Some would claim that other early works, notably *A Streetcar Named Desire* and *Cat on a Hot Tin Roof,* are more "complete" as works of literature. Here they are judging these plays against the standard Williams set in his first successful drama, forgetting that *The Glass Menagerie* opened the drama to new dimensions of reality hitherto unexplored on the American stage.

That Williams was on the vanguard of the theater is a point made by a number of critics. Arthur Miller, who functions as both a playwright and critic, has written that in the mid-1940s, *The Glass Menagerie* represented a change in the direction of the drama: "It is usually forgotten what a revolution his first great success meant to the New York theatre. *The Glass Menagerie* in one stroke lifted lyricism to its highest level in our theatre's history, but it broke new ground in another way. What was new in Tennessee Williams was his rhapsodic insistence that form serve his utterance rather than dominating and cramping it. In him the American theatre found, perhaps for the first time, an eloquence and amplitude of feeling."[8]

In his production notes to *The Glass Menagerie* Williams makes the point that he conceived of the theater as a vital experience that realism virtually had destroyed. He calls for a "new, plastic theatre" because "truth, life, or reality is an organic thing which the poetic imagination can represent." By using the language of poetry, as Miller suggests, Williams revived the drama. Esther Merle Jackson finds the "poetic vision" at the heart of most of Williams's plays. In *The Glass Menagerie* she finds "little if any action in the Aristotelian sense; that is, there is in this vision no strict pattern of causal development, from beginning to end. For in the lyric moment, action is aesthetic; it is the growth of understanding. Through his poet figure, the dramatist invites the spectator to share his fragmentary vision."[9] His approach is "poetic" rather than "realistic." The details of the script, as scholars often have written, reveal how Williams as poet uses the symbols of glass and motion pictures, as well as poetic speech patterns. But there are many patterns, cadences, symbols, and motifs at work in the play. There is the photograph of the absent father, referred to throughout the play as "the telephone man who fell in love with long distance." The reader might also consider the poetic value of those forty-four illuminations or images that Williams intended to be shown on a screen at key moments.

Character analysis presents another fruitful approach. Amanda is a particularly engaging subject as she neurotically needles Tom and caustically upbraids Laura. Is she a caricature of the faded southern belle who lives in an imaginary world of suitors and social halls? Critics often have shared Tom's angry judgment that she is an "ugly— babbling old—witch." (scene 3). Yet what are we to make of those occasions when Amanda shows depth and understanding, as we note in her rapprochement with Tom in scene 4? And what about Tom? Is there any moral depth in this daydreaming and movie-addicted son who finally puts his own welfare above that of his mother and sister?

An advantage Williams offers to modern interpreters is that many of his plays are inhabited by characters who bear striking resemblance. To study the "neurotic" Amanda, for example, is to prepare oneself for the "schizophrenic" Blanche of *A Streetcar Named Desire*. Laura is prefigured by the shy central figure in his early short story "Portrait of a Girl in Glass." The ambiguous relationship between Tom and Laura is similar to that of a brother and sister in *The Two-Character Play* (1967). Such continuities and connections encourage readers to propose new interpretations and draw conclusions that often are provocative.[10]

To probe questions such as those I have raised is to engage in interpretation—that is, literary criticism. Above all else, good criticism demands fair-mindedness and intellectual rigor. One who answers these questions will be able to tackle the larger issue of the drama's focus and meaning. Clearly the final word about Williams and his first successful play has not been written. As a great work of the imagination, it probably always will remain like Laura's menagerie, forever offering new and interesting reflections for all who bring to bear the mind's best light.

a reading

CHAPTER 4

Whose Play Is It?

All of us share a common experience when we begin to discuss *The Glass Menagerie*. Sooner or later we face the question, "Whose play is it?" We deal with it eventually because it happens to be a very good question. To discuss the matter leads one to speculate not only about the author's point of view but about the meaning of the play itself. One who answers the question should consider the full range of possibilities.

Could it be Laura's play, since so much of Tom's memory deals with his sister and her delicate collection of glass, to which the title refers. On the other hand, one might argue that the play belongs to Jim, the gentleman caller, the character who momentarily transforms the Wingfield's apartment into a cheerful-looking place. The anticipation of Jim dominates much of the dialogue, and once he concludes his visit, the play ends. Or could the central character be Tom Wingfield who narrates the events? This character speaks the first and last words, after all.

More often than not, the answer comes swiftly: the play belongs to Amanda. This response has been typical of reviewers of the drama since it was first produced. Early notices in Chicago and New York focused attention on the character whose mere presence in a scene tends to dominate it. In his review, Joseph Wood Krutch wrote of "the terrible old woman who is the central figure." And the critic John Mason Brown concluded that the "evening's performance—more accurately the season's—is Miss Taylor's."[1] Miss Taylor established a benchmark for future portrayals of Amanda by some of the most distinguished actresses of the twentieth century. Foster Hirsch's introduction of 1979, *A Portrait of the Artist: The Plays of Tennessee Williams*, summarizes a commonly held position:

> Tom's mother, Amanda, is the central character. . . . Amanda is one
> of the playwright's most vivid Southern belles, but she differs from
> Blanche Du Bois or Alma Winemiller in being remarkably practical.
> She is very much aware of the world, and her main goal in life is to
> communicate that awareness to her painfully shy daughter.[2]

Another reason the mother stands out in discussions about this drama concerns her role as the instigator of action. It is Amanda who sends Laura to business college to learn a marketable skill. Once this plan fails, she begins preparing for a gentleman caller—a potential husband—for Laura. It is Amanda who sends Tom off to work each day because his job is necessary for the family's economic survival, at least until Laura is married. Finally it is Amanda who badgers Tom throughout the play until he angrily "descended the steps of this fire-escape for a last time" (123). Viewed in this light, Amanda has a fragile menagerie composed of two children, one of whom manages to escape.

Scholarly interpreters of the play sometimes link Amanda with other dominant heroines of Williams. Several introductions to the playwright discuss Amanda as one among several of his major female characters. Typically she is compared with Blanche DuBois of *A Streetcar Named Desire*, with Alma Winemiller of *Summer and Smoke*, and with female protagonists in later plays. The following excerpt from a critical essay demonstrates the logic of viewing Amanda as the original model for a kind of heroine in Williams's works (notice that the author views Amanda as one who represents "a retreat into illusion" and who is "unable to love"):

> In seven plays written in a twenty year period, Williams uses essentially the same dramatic situation. A woman is presented at a moment when frustration has led to a crisis. She has only two possible ways of acting: to face reality or to retreat into illusion. . . . Between 1940 and 1960 Williams moves from the delineation of women who live in illusion and hence are unable to love to the delineation of women who accept the reality of their lives and become concerned and compassionate or at least ready for unselfish love.[3]

While one can gain valuable insight into Williams's female characters through such analyses, the fact remains that Amanda, first of all, is a character in a particular play. Before generalizing about how Williams's heroines function comparatively, our first task is to deal with the roles of all characters involved in the plays. Specifically in *The Glass Menagerie* the character of Amanda must be seen in the context of her action onstage. In fact, although she is a dominant personality, one can make a case that another character plays the central role.

Contrary to the majority opinion offered by critics, Tom's role is pivotal. He is both the narrator and a major character. Were Tom a character alone, Amanda would own the play without question. Because he functions as narrator, however, Tom establishes a relationship with his audience. He invites us into his memory of a past that is peculiar to him, a memory inhabited by characters named Amanda, Laura, Jim, and Tom. These characters function in a world of imagery and meaning peculiar to Tom's imagination.

Tom's invitation is a clever one. Describing himself as a magician, he pricks the audience's imagination by describing his peculiar sleight of hand: "But I am the opposite of a stage magician. He gives you illusion that has the appearance of truth. I give you truth in the pleasant disguise of illusion" (4). Immediately we are forced to accept Tom's central role. He is our guide to life in lower-middle-class St. Louis during the Great Depression. He carries us beyond the ash heaps and dance halls and into the small apartment he once shared with his mother and sister. He explains that the play is not realistic but "sentimental" because it is his memory, after all.

We might think of Tom as a modern Dante, whose *Inferno* segment of the *Divine Comedy* begins: "Midway in our life's journey, I went astray from the straight road and woke to find myself alone in a dark wood."[4] Tom also has lost his way along life's journey, and he has poignant memories of events leading up to his departure. These memories follow him wherever he journeys "attempting to find in motion what was lost in space." Like Dante, Tom's memory is replete with images of people he had known earlier in his life.

Dante's world of the imagination is much larger than his native Florence, Italy. It has a cast of thousands, most of them lost souls bearing names familiar to those who read history and literature of the period. Williams, on the other hand, largely confines himself to contemporary events: the Great Depression, the Spanish Civil War, political unrest, and contemporary social conditions. Williams establishes the drama's context unmistakably in the 1930s, "when the huge middle class of America was matriculating in a school for the blind." As a poet, Tom also tends to remember events symbolically, and so he describes Jim as a kind of savior from a "world of reality" in which the Wingfields do not live. His absent father's photographic image (the man who "skipped the light fantastic out of town") is a visible symbol throughout most of the play.

As Dante passes through the inferno, he relies on Virgil as his guide. But Tom, the loner, is both pilgrim and interpreter as he carries us through his private hell. As the opening monologue makes clear, it is Tom's story. Without him the magic cannot begin. As if to underscore the importance of Tom's role in the action onstage, Williams subtly begins scene 1:

AMANDA (*Calling*): Tom?

TOM: Yes, Mother.

AMANDA: We can't say grace until you come to the table!

TOM: Coming, Mother. (*He bows slightly and with-*

Whose Play Is It?

draws, reappearing a few moments later in his place at the table.)

Remarkably Tom-as-narrator carefully maintains his distance from Tom-as-character. For example, as a victim of Amanda's constant correcting and biting sarcasm, the character Tom both winces and responds in kind onstage. As narrator, however, Tom maintains a kind of polite aloofness just short of detachment. Obviously he cares about what happens onstage. His job, however, is to focus our attention on the order of events and their significance to him.

As a character he can speak sarcastically about his mother. But as narrator he is more objective and occasionally concludes his comments with a twist of ironic humor, further detaching himself from the action: As the third scene opens, Tom prepares us to follow the events that lead to the climax of his life at home: the preparation for a gentleman caller.

An evening at home rarely passed without some allusion to this image, this spectre, this hope. . . .

Even when he wasn't mentioned, his presence hung in Mother's preoccupied look and in my sister's frightened, apologetic manner—hung like a sentence passed upon the Wingfields!

Mother was a woman of action as well as words.

Audiences often laugh at this point because they also have grown a bit weary of her steady stream of advice and complaint, not to mention those lengthy accounts of her golden days in Blue Mountain.

Some critics and even directors, deciding that the play belongs to Amanda, have proposed that Tom's narrations should be eliminated. Finding these sections distracting, they have suggested that the play would make a smoother production without them. Then the play would focus more directly on Amanda's menagerie of children, and it would undoubtedly lead to a more moving experience, at least in terms of sentimentality. But consider what such a production would lose. More significant than anything else, it would lose the sense of distance—the perspective—with which Tom tells his story. A great deal of time has elapsed since that heated moment of his past when he decided to leave home. Then, face flushed with anger, he argued with his mother vehemently. Now he calmly shares his story with the audience, possessing the calm certainty of a stage magician. Wearing the clothing of a sailor, he speaks directly to the audience with cool detachment. He has gained a perspective provided by his extensive travels in the world and, even more, by his longer journey through time.

It is Tom's perspective as narrator that allows him to introduce and interpret the characters. For example, in the play, Tom's friend at the warehouse, Jim O'Connor, provides him with a way of keeping an agreement he made with his mother. But in his narration Tom explains how Jim, in spite of his own difficulties along the road of success, functions as a symbol of hope for the Wingfields. It is this same perspective that allows Tom to control his own self-portrayal. As narrator Tom makes Amanda the object of some clever lines. But the character Tom does not possess that sense of detachment. At the end of the third scene, his ironic touch gives way to a heavy hand in a vicious argument with his mother, prompted by her refusal to believe that Tom in fact goes to the movies as often as he claims:

> I'm going to opium dens! Yes, opium dens, dens of vice and criminals' hang-outs, Mother. I've joined the Hogan gang, I'm a hired assassin, I carry a tommy-gun in a violin case! I run a string of cat-houses in the Valley! They call me Killer, Killer Wingfield, I'm leading a double-life, a simple, honest warehouse worker by day, by night a dynamic *czar* of the *underworld, Mother.* I go to gambling casinos, I spin away fortunes on the roulette table! I wear a patch over one eye and a false mustache, sometimes I put on green whiskers. On those occasions they call me—*El Diablo!* Oh, I could tell you things to make you sleepless! My enemies plan to dynamite this place. They're going to blow us all sky-high some night! I'll be glad, very happy, and so will you! You'll go up, up on a broomstick, over Blue Mountain with seventeen gentlemen callers! You ugly—babbling old—*witch.*

As if to underscore Tom's loss of control, Williams has him struggle to put on his overcoat and to hurl it in frustration against the shelf containing Laura's glass menagerie. The scene ends shortly after the mother's wounded comment:

> I won't speak to you—until you apologize! (*She crosses through portieres and draws them together behind her. Tom is left with* LAURA. LAURA *clings weakly to the mantel with her face averted.* TOM *stares at her stupidly for a moment. Then he crosses to shelf. Drops awkwardly on his knees to collect the fallen glass, glancing at* LAURA *as if he would speak but couldn't.*)

As narrator Tom speaks rhythmically, as though reading passages from his poems. He turns phrases deftly: "Their eyes had failed them, or they had failed their eyes" (5). He even acknowledges "a poet's weakness for symbols" in his use of the gentleman caller "as a symbol: he is the long delayed but always expected something that we live for." The one who is never expected is "our father who left us a long time ago. He was a telephone man who fell in love with long distances."

The character Tom writes poetry, but we never hear him read it. For the most part his lines are delivered in everyday language. (There are a few exceptions, as in "I'm tired of the *movies* and I am *about* to *move!*" [scene 6, 76]). In fact Amanda's speeches contain more images and figures of speech than Tom's. Amanda's memorable jonquil speech in the sixth scene can be read as an extended poem:

> Something I've resurrected from that old trunk! Styles haven't changed so terribly much after all. . . .
> Now just look at your mother!
> This is the dress in which I led the cotillion. Won the cakewalk twice at Sunset Hill, wore one spring to the Governor's ball in Jackson!
> See how I sashayed around the ballroom, Laura?
> (*She raises her skirt and does a mincing step around the room.*)
> I wore it on Sundays for my gentlemen callers! I had it on the day I met your father—
> I had malaria fever all that spring. The change of climate from East Tennessee to the Delta—weakened resistance—I had a little temperature all the time—not enough to be serious—just enough to

make me restless and giddy! Invitations poured in—parties all over the Delta! "Stay in bed," said Mother, "you have a fever!"—but I just wouldn't.—I took quinine but kept on going, going! Evenings, dances!—Afternoons, long, long rides! Picnics—lovely! So lovely, that country in May.—All lacy with dogwood, literally flooded with jonquils!—That was the spring I had the craze for jonquils. Jonquils became an absolute obsession. Mother said, "Honey, there's no more room for jonquils." And still I kept on bringing in more jonquils. Whenever, wherever I saw them, I'd say, "Stop! Stop! I see jonquils!" I made the young men help me gather the jonquils! It was a joke, Amanda and her jonquils! Finally there were no more vases to hold them, every available space was filled with jonquils. No vases to hold them? All right, I'll hold them myself! And then I (*She stops in front of the picture.* MUSIC) met your father!

Malaria fever and jonquils and then—this—boy—

In a perceptive article, Frank Durham treats this and a number of other passages in the play as poetry. The selection just quoted is an excellent example: "It has the patterned construction of a poem, its rhythms capture the emotions of its speaker, it embodies the comic-pathetic ideal of the gracious past, and it relies on floral imagery to enhance its resonance as poetry."[5]

If Tom-as-character is not impressed by his mother's poetic utterances, Tom-as-narrator reflects her strong influence in most of his narrations and soliloquies. The influence stops, however, at the level of language. The narrator is detached from the scenes he describes. The sense of detachment is an extremely important component in his role as an objective observer. Indeed, a great challenge facing the actor who portrays Tom is precisely how to deliver the narratives lines. The first to portray Tom onstage, Eddie Dowling, established a precedent of sorts in his opening performance in 1944. He spoke the lines as though he were reading them. John Malkovich incorporates precisely this technique, even whispering and mumbling some of the narration, as if speaking to himself, in Paul Newman's motion picture film of 1987.

To observe Tom portrayed as a detached narrator may surprise one who has read the play before seeing it. It both surprised and disturbed the drama critic, Stark Young, who wrote of Dowling's original performance: "He speaks his Narrator scenes plainly and serviceably by which, I think, they are made to seem to be a mistake on the playwright's part, a mistake to include them at all; for they seem extraneous and tiresome in the midst of the play's emotional current."[6] To follow Young's advice may give the play a stronger sense of continuity, but it would rob the play of its uniqueness.

It is Tom who stands between the audience and the action. It is Tom who provides a perspective that allows him to transcend limitations imposed by events onstage. Yet he is never completely detached. He shares with us a memory of his life that time cannot erase. Addressing his audience at perfectly timed moments, he deliberately reveals that his sleight of hand is no mere illusion. At the play's conclusion we realize that Tom has turned his memory into our own.

CHAPTER 5

The Pleasant Disguise of Illusion: A View of the Characters

THE NARRATOR AS MAGICIAN

In the opening monologue Tom describes himself as a sleight of hand artist: "I have tricks in my pocket. I have things up my sleeve" (4). Yet he is not a typical stage magician intent on deceiving his audience. Instead of presenting illusion that looks real, he says, "I give you truth in the pleasant disguise of illusion" (4). If his object is truth, then what is his subject? Himself. More precisely, Tom Wingfield's subject is his life before he began to practice his kind of magic. He wishes to explore those forces that have shaped him. If Tom were a historian, he might focus on some of the significant events he refers to in his "social background of the play," but he is not a historian. If Tom were a psychoanalyst, he might probe deeply those human relationships he experienced as a child and young man, but he is not a psychoanalyst.

As he stands before us at the beginning of this drama, Tom is a magician. His particular forte lies in the complex realm of memory. Before our very eyes he turns back the clock and mysteriously transforms the theater into a scene from his past. He performs on a stage that the playwright has prepared especially for him. The set allows us to see the Wingfield apartment's interior and exterior at the same time. Even as we observe events unfold in the dining room, we are ever aware that the apartment entrance is a fire escape.

Tom also manipulates his audience with music: "In memory everything seems to happen to music. That explains the fiddle in the wings" (5). The production notes describe the tune, "The Glass Menagerie," in detail. It was composed with Tom's magic in mind: "This tune is like circus music, not when you are on the grounds or in the immediate vicinity of the parade, but when you are at some distance and very likely thinking of something else." The music will appear between each episode, especially when the play focuses on Tom's sister, the delicate keeper of the fragile collection of glass.

He reinforces the aspect of memory by using lighting especially designed to capture the emotional meaning of events. The interior is dim for a reason: to focus better on the subjective meaning, the emotional content, of his presentation. To flood the stage with light would destroy the atmosphere of memory. Sometimes in shafts and sometimes in pools, light functions in a manner reminiscent of the painter El Greco, whose "figures are radiant" in an atmosphere that is "relatively dusky," Williams explains in his production notes.

In addition to the see-through set, the evocative music, and the dim lighting, Tom takes advantage of another device designed for this production alone: a projection screen. One does not notice the screen because it is also a section of the wall between the front room and the dining area. Yet one cannot miss the forty-four images and titles that appear on the screen throughout the play.

Although Williams intended to use the screen projections in the stage production, his director found them distracting and convinced him to delete them. Having witnessed the "extraordinary power of Miss [Laurette] Taylor's performance," Williams found "it suitable to have the utmost simplicity in the physical production," he wrote in his production notes. In both the original and the reading versions of the script, however, Williams included the device in order "to give accent to certain values in each scene. Each scene contains a particular point (or several) which is structurally the most important. . . . The legend or image upon the screen will strengthen the effect of what is merely allusion in the writing and allow the primary point to be made more simply and lightly than if the entire responsibility were on the spoken lines." Occasionally, as in the 1983 revival in New York and in some European productions, the screen has been used effectively.

When Tom explains that he uses illusion as a "pleasant disguise" for truth, he brings to bear all of the techniques and devices mentioned above (not to mention the photograph of his "ineluctably smiling" father that magically lights up at precisely the right moment in the play). Now the final point to be made about Tom's role as a magician is this: he is so successful in his presentation that we soon have forgotten about his trickery. How easily and quickly have we moved into the world of his memory.

Tom broadly hints that the social context of the play implicates society, perhaps even the audience. Without pausing to reflect on the bold social implications of his opening monologue, however, Tom begins presenting those illusions he suggests will lead us toward the truth. The audience shares much in common with the characters on-stage. Tom's opening remarks indicate that members of the audience should be alert to his preference for irony, for the master of deception deftly shows how craftily all of us weave our own deceptions. Tom also challenges the audience to see beyond the illusion onstage—beyond even our own self-deception—and to find the truth he has to offer.

Ironically what the playwright reveals is a cast of characters caught up in illusions of their own making. All of them—his mother Amanda, his sister Laura, his friend Jim, even the earlier version of himself—have built their lives on insubstantial premises of deception. Each one, however, also presents a glimpse of the truth. Combined, these glimpses form a larger vision of life's meaning. It is this vision that lifts the play beyond the limitations imposed by the stage presentation—even a magician's stage, fully enhanced with a unique set, artful lighting, theme music, and screen projections. Since we are subject to an inverted form of magic, however, we must appreciate the illusion before we can envision the truth embodied in these four characters.

AMANDA

In scene 1, after the Wingfields finish the evening meal, Amanda pretends she is a servant and cleans the dishes, telling Laura she needs "to stay fresh and pretty—for gentlemen callers" (8). Ignoring Laura's comment that she does not expect any visitors, Amanda begins a familiar reverie about "one Sunday afternoon in Blue Mountain." Tom tells Laura that he knows "what's coming!" But Laura insists that Amanda be allowed the privilege of cultivating the illusion: "She loves to tell it" (8).

Amanda's version of the past is both a private and a public myth. She has fond personal memories of her childhood and youth in Blue Mountain. She recollects this community in the Mississippi Delta as the home of a number of prosperous cotton farmers, merchants, and landholders. There she participated in the social and cultural activities, which she found rewarding. There were cotillions, cake walks, and occasions for entertaining her many gentlemen callers.

While it is fruitless to question the truthfulness of her reminiscences, one should note that she speaks as though she had been reared in the antebellum South. In the first scene she wants "sister" to play the role of "the lady this time, and I'll be the darky" (8). Laura's role, as Amanda fantasizes it, is that of the southern belle. When Amanda was a young woman, she says the seventeen gentlemen callers forced her family "to send the nigger over to bring in folding chairs from the parish house" (9). One might think she grew up during the days of plantation slavery. In fact she is using the language of a myth that had wide currency during her youth. She certainly did not invent the myth.

Although they mean a great deal to her, these conversational diversions reflect neither mental imbalance nor idiosyncratic behavior. She inherited a view of the world that inspired many who lived in the Deep South in the late nineteenth and early twentieth centuries. Indeed in the middle and late 1930s, the myth of the antebellum South permeates a best-selling novel by Margaret Mitchell, *Gone with the Wind*. Amanda refers to this book as she telephones a friend, attempting to sell a magazine subscription:

> You remember how *Gone with the Wind* took everybody by storm? You simply couldn't go out if you hadn't read it. All everybody talked was Scarlett O'Hara. Well this is a book that critics already compare to *Gone with the Wind*. It's the *Gone with the Wind* of the post–World War generation!

Amanda's myth of the Old South, of course, influences no one onstage, though it does give rise to one of Tom's humorous remarks in the first scene:

TOM: How did you entertain those gentlemen callers?
AMANDA: I understood the art of conversation!
TOM: I bet you could talk.

The stage directions note the impact the myth has on Amanda: "Her eyes lift, her face glows, her voice becomes rich and elegiac" (scene 1). Both Tom and Laura give her the pleasure of these moments of reverie. Later in the play Jim O'Connor also is impressed by the myth of Blue Mountain. Observing Amanda's "girlish Southern vivacity" and "unexpected outlay of social charm" near the end of the sixth scene, Jim "reacts very warmly. Grins and chuckles, is altogether won over." In spite of the vigor with which she pursues her illusions, clearly Amanda is deceiving herself. Hers is a mythology not of this world, a mythology that works only in a fictional Tara.

Critics commonly have misinterpreted the role of Amanda and thus have distorted the meaning of the play. Some refer to it as a tragedy about a woman completely out of touch with reality. Joseph

The Pleasant Disguise of Illusion

Wood Krutch summarizes that Amanda is a heroine although "an absurd and pathetic widow" who is "defeated by a crude and pushing modernity which neither understands nor respects her dream of gentility."[1] Amanda is an older-generation southerner who, as she tells Jim in scene 6, "wasn't prepared for what the future brought me." But she is more than a stereotypical matron who is out of touch with reality. To view her exclusively in this light is to see the mere illusion created by the playwright. Amanda is a complex character, and she possesses the gift of insight that lifts her above the role of stereotype.

Amanda realizes that her shy and retiring daughter needs to overcome self-pity and gain independence. The task is all important and, in Amanda's view, demands sacrifice. Thus she accepts a demeaning job at Famous and Barr's Department Store demonstrating ladies' undergarments in order to pay for Laura's tuition at Rubicam's Business College. She also wants Tom to have a brighter future, which will allow him to realize his talents. This is why she encourages him to spend his evenings at night school rather than at the movies. In scene 5 Amanda tells Tom her deepest wish: "Success and happiness for my precious children! I wish for that whenever there's a moon, and when there isn't a moon, I wish for it, too."

Amanda's solution of suggesting that Tom find a gentleman caller for Laura may seem extreme. Some interpreters view this request as her frantic effort to impose the image of her youth upon Laura. Yet this move should be viewed as Amanda's last resort—the only solution she can devise for a crisis Laura created when she surreptitiously dropped out of her secretarial course just as she had dropped out of high school. If Amanda appears desperate, she certainly has a legitimate reason. She also reveals self-awareness when she tells Laura: "I'm just bewildered . . . by life" (15).

In his character description of Amanda, Williams carefully makes the point that she possesses some depth of feeling and understanding:

> A little woman of great but confused vitality clinging frantically to another time and place. Her characterization must be carefully created, not copied from type. She is not paranoiac, but her life is paranoia. There is much to admire in Amanda, and as much to love

and pity as there is to laugh at. Certainly she has endurance and a kind of heroism, and though her foolishness makes her unwittingly cruel at times, there is tenderness in her slight person.

With this view in mind, we should notice Amanda in scene 4 after Tom apologizes for his caustic treatment of her on the previous evening. Williams indicates that "Ave Maria" should be played softly underneath the confessional exchange between mother and son:

AMANDA: My devotion has made me a witch and so I make myself hateful to my children!

TOM: *No, you don't.*

AMANDA: I worry so much, don't sleep, it makes me nervous!

TOM: I understand that.

AMANDA: I've had to put up a solitary battle all these years. But you're my right-hand bower! Don't fall down, don't fail!

TOM: I try, Mother.

Amanda continues, explaining to Tom that she can understand, if not approve of, his restlessness:

I know your ambitions do not lie in the warehouse, that like everybody in the whole wide world—you've had to—make sacrifices, but—Tom—Tom—life's not easy, it calls for—Spartan endurance!

Now we see Amanda without benefit of her own distracting illusions. It is her way of acknowledging the core of truth inside all her talk about those gentlemen callers. The sons of planters might have given her the security of position and privilege. She probably could have married Duncan J. Fitzhugh, "the Wolf of Wall Street," the man with "the Midas touch, whatever he touched turned to gold!" She confesses, perhaps unintentionally, to Jim:

I married no planter! I married a man who worked for the telephone company! That gallantly smiling gentleman over there! (*Points to the picture*) A telephone man who fell in love with long distance!— Now he travels and I don't even know where!—

The Pleasant Disguise of Illusion

More than anyone else in the drama, it is Amanda who always seems to reap the bitter consequences of deception. Amanda realizes she has been deceived, and not only by the telephone company employee she married. She also has been the victim of deception by the daughter who pretended to be attending secretarial school, and she will discover deception by the son who fails to pay the light bill, and unwittingly by Laura's gentleman caller who is already engaged. The critical deception originated with the man she agreed to marry long ago. He once offered something of far greater importance than mere security. In her confessional talk with Tom in scene 4, she tells him: "There's so many things in my heart that I cannot describe to you! I've never told you but I—*loved* your father." Her despair fundamentally rests on a decision she made as a young woman. However, we know that she could have made a decision even worse than marrying Mr. Wingfield: she could have married someone she did not love.

What, then, is the truth about Amanda? Try as we may, we never can strip away her disguise, so we seek the truth about her even as we acknowledge her falsehood. Seen through the eyes of a restless Tom, her deception at times seems larger than life. Yet it is Tom finally who reveals the truth in his memory of his mother: She is an extremely complex character who reflects the extremely complex nature of human love. As if to underscore a sympathetic interpretation of Amanda at the conclusion of the play, Tom remembers her as follows:

> AMANDA appears to be making a comforting speech to LAURA who is huddled upon the sofa. Now that we cannot hear the mother's speech, her silliness is gone and she has dignity and tragic beauty. . . . AMANDA's gestures are slow and graceful, almost dance-like, as she comforts her daughter. At the end of her speech she glances a moment at the father's picture—then withdraws through the portieres (123).

This, then, is the true Amanda. This is the one who finally appears through the magic of Tom's illusion. The closing pantomime profoundly projects this image of enduring love that radiantly fills the stage until Laura blows out her candles. Amanda comforts Laura with a depth of understanding known especially by those who have the capacity to love. The image lingers forever in Tom's memory as he journeys through time.

LAURA

Laura lives in a world of illusion. Her existence revolves around her collection of transparent glass animals, which she can order and control. The menagerie is her means of escaping from family tensions and her own sense of futility. So is the Victrola, which she plays whenever she wants to forget the unpleasantness of her life in the apartment. Williams's description of Laura is particularly helpful:

> Amanda, having failed to establish contact with reality, continues to live vitally in her illusions, but Laura's situation is even graver. A childhood illness has left her crippled, one leg slightly shorter than the other, and held in a brace. This defect need not be more than suggested on the stage. Stemming from this, Laura's separation increases till she is like a piece of her own glass collection, too exquisitely fragile to move from the shelf.

At the beginning of scene 2, we see Laura washing and polishing her collection. The stage directions read: "Amanda appears on the fire-escape steps. At the sound of her ascent, Laura catches her breath, thrusts the bowl of ornaments away and seats herself stiffly before the diagram of the typewriter keyboard as though it held her spellbound." Her mother soon will reveal that she knows Laura long has been engaged in an elaborate effort to deceive her:

LAURA: Hello, Mother, I was—(*She makes a nervous gesture toward the chart on the wall.* AMANDA *leans against the shut door and stares at* LAURA *with a martyred look.*)

AMANDA: Deception? Deception?

40

The Pleasant Disguise of Illusion

Soon Amanda reveals that today she has discovered that Laura long ago had dropped out of Rubicam's Business College, having experienced an embarrassing seizure of fear when she took her first speed test. Laura acknowledges her deception immediately, saying that instead of going to college she had walked in the park, visited the art museum, or the "Jewel-box, that big glass house where they raise the tropical flowers."

> AMANDA: So what are we going to do the rest of our lives? Stay home and watch the parades go by? Amuse ourselves with the glass menagerie, darling? Eternally play those worn-out phonograph records your father left as a painful reminder of him? (scene 2)

The answers to Amanda's rhetorical questions are the same: yes, yes, yes, and yes. Laura has no plan for the rest of her life. She has accepted her isolation as hopeless. Each day she repeats a routine of caring for her menagerie and playing music, occasionally interrupted by domestic chores and conversations with her mother and brother. Although Laura cultivates her illusions, she attempts no further deception after her mother discovers the truth about her short tenure at Rubicam's Business College.

Although Laura's life is caught up in self-sustained illusions, she acknowledges her situation freely. She has given up trying to be "normal." A dropout of high school as well as business college, she apparently is prepared to lead a life of dependency. Her resignation perhaps explains why Laura allows Amanda to tell, again and again, those familiar accounts of her youth in the Mississippi Delta long ago when Amanda received the attention of so many gentlemen callers. Laura begs an impatient Tom, "Let her tell it. . . . She loves to tell it" (8). Laura knows how important illusions can be as one seeks to cope with pressures of daily living.

There is a sense of honesty in Laura's attitude, the kind of honesty one sometimes finds among those awaiting death. She does not want to become involved in life as Amanda would have her. She is afflicted with a profound shyness, and she is afraid even to attempt to overcome it. The mere thought of social activity makes her nauseous. Once Amanda realizes that Laura will never learn skills necessary for employment, she decides that Laura's only hope is to find a husband:

AMANDA: Girls that aren't cut out for business careers usually wind up married to some nice man. . . . Sister, that's what you'll do!

LAURA: But, Mother—

AMANDA: Yes?

LAURA: I'm crippled!

AMANDA: Nonsense! Laura, I've told you never, never to use that word. Why, you're not crippled, you just have a little defect— hardly noticeable, even! When people have some slight disadvantage like that, they cultivate other things to make up for it—develop charm—and vivacity—and—*charm!* That's all you have to do!

Laura is not a willing candidate for Amanda's school of charm, even when she helps her mother prepare the apartment and herself for the gentleman caller. As the moment approaches, Amanda wraps two powder puffs in handkerchiefs and stuffs them in Laura's bosom. Amanda calls them "Gay Deceivers":

LAURA: I won't wear them!

AMANDA: You will!

LAURA: Why should I?

AMANDA: Because, to be painfully honest, your chest is flat.

LAURA: You make it seem like we were setting a trap.

AMANDA: All pretty girls are a trap, a pretty trap, and men expect them to be.

Laura's favorite glass animal, the unicorn, is a symbol for herself: fragile and different. Her conversation about the unicorn with Jim reveals much that is meaningful in the play, including how she visualizes herself in the larger realm of society:

> JIM: Unicorns, aren't they extinct in the modern world?
>
> LAURA: I know!
>
> JIM: Poor little fellow, he must feel sort of lonesome.
>
> LAURA: Well, if he does he doesn't complain about it. He stays on a shelf with some horses that don't have horns and all of them seem to get along nicely together. (scene 7)

Laura interprets the unicorn as a symbol of her condition. She endows it with her own introversion and, like the unicorn, accepts her lonely isolation and "doesn't complain about it." Her major task is to protect herself, as though she were made of glass: "Oh, be careful—if you breathe, it breaks!" (105). This symbolic identity is reinforced near the end of play when Jim's clumsy dancing with her causes the unicorn to fall and break off its horn.

The accident prefigures Jim's announcement that he is engaged and will not visit the Wingfield apartment again. Williams writes: "The holy candles in the altar of Laura's face have been snuffed out. There is a look of almost infinite desolation." After giving Jim the symbol of herself, now broken, she can only move nearer to what Amanda refers to earlier that evening as "the everlasting darkness" (124). Laura once again has played the role of victim, and at the play's conclusion it is she who extinguishes the light. The act is Laura's bleak affirmation of truth—her ultimate withdrawal into the dark of the shadows of herself.

JIM

Among all the characters who inhabit the collection of plays by Tennessee Williams, Jim O'Connor stands alone. Several works reveal characters who embody some of the materialistic values of modern capitalism. Nowhere else, however, does the playwright allow the materialist to touch the very soul of a major character. Jim is especially well drawn in the text, although some directors present him simply. Williams's notes on the characters describe Jim in a single phrase: "A nice, ordinary, young man." Often productions, including Paul Newman's motion picture film of 1987, have given us Jim as a clean-cut, up-and-coming lad who happens to be in the wrong place at the wrong time when he visits the Wingfields. But can Jim be "simply" portrayed as "nice" and "ordinary"? Well, "simply" is out of the question for Jim O'Connor as Williams draws him in the reading text of the play. Furthermore the adjectives *nice* and *ordinary* are loaded with ambiguity, if not pejorative implications, in Williams's dictionary.

Jim's portrait reflects extremely careful planning and execution by the playwright. While the narrator's view of him ultimately fixes his identity, we must appreciate the illusion of his character. First, we see Jim in terms of his relationship to other characters. Second, we see him as he sees himself. Third, we see him as he appears under the scrutiny of Tom, the magician-as-narrator. The third view is the truth that appears in all these illusions.

Seen through the eyes of Amanda, Jim fundamentally is a potential husband for Laura. Just as he embodies Laura's only hope for a future, he also is Amanda's only hope for fulfilling one of her major duties as a mother. She explains to Tom that once Laura "has got somebody to take care of her, married, a home of her own, independent—why you'll be free to go wherever you please, on land, on sea, whichever way the wind blows you!" (42).

Amanda had asked Tom to find a young man "that's clean-living—doesn't drink and—ask him out for sister!" (43). When Tom announces that he has found a caller who intends to have dinner with the Wingfields the following evening, Amanda regrets the short notice but quickly begins to size up Laura's prospective beau. Learning his name is Irish (O'Connor), she decides to serve fish (salmon loaf with Durkee's dressing). Tom tells Amanda that Jim's salary as a shipping clerk in the shoe warehouse is twenty dollars a month more than his.

He also reveals that Jim attends night school where he pursues his interests in radio engineering and public speaking. She assumes that he does not drink since Tom has no knowledge of Jim's personal habits. This is all Tom tells Amanda about the gentlemen caller before he arrives. That he will be the one to answer her prayers is Amanda's fondest wish.

Jim does not realize that the invitation to visit the Wingfields is part of Amanda's deception, her trap. Tom had not told him that he has a sister: "I just said, why don't you come and have dinner with us? He said okay and that was the whole conversation" (57). Amanda replies with typical optimism that "he'll know about Laura when he gets here. When he sees how lovely and sweet and pretty she is, he'll thank his lucky stars he was asked to dinner" (58). In a few moments as they watch a "little silver slipper of a moon," Amanda tells Laura to wish for "Happiness! Good fortune!" (60). She speaks with "voice trembling and her eyes suddenly filling with tears." At this moment we can recall Tom's opening description of the gentleman caller: "I am using this character also as a symbol; he is the long delayed but always expected something that we live for" (5).

Laura views the arrival of the gentleman caller with trepidation, especially when she discovers that he is the one person she secretly had idolized at Soldan High School. In scene 3 Laura discusses Jim with Amanda, responding to her mother's question: "Haven't you ever liked some boy?" As the screen projection reveals "JIM AS HIGH-SCHOOL HERO BEARING A SILVER CUP," Laura shows Amanda the yearbook that chronicles some of his achievements as the lead singer in the senior class operetta and as champion debater. She also recalls that he had a girlfriend named Emily Meisenbach who "never struck me, though, as being sincere" (21). Laura explains that Jim never knew her name; however, he called her "Blue Roses." (When he once asked her why she had been absent from school, he misconstrued her answer—"pleurosis." "So that's what he always called me after that" [20].) Later when Laura realizes that their dinner guest likely will be the same Jim O'Connor, she tells Amanda, "You'll have to excuse me, I won't come to the table." The screen legend we see immediately before

Laura opens the door for Tom and Jim summarizes her condition: "TERROR!"

What is Tom's view of his fellow employee at the shoe warehouse? First and foremost, Jim's visit helps Tom keep an agreement he had made with Amanda after their reconciliation in scene 4. Since Tom already has made plans to become a seaman imminently, his procurement of Jim is a parting gesture. He makes the appointment with little difficulty and never considers that the short notice will severely inconvenience his mother. Of course, he assumes that soon he will not have to consider her and Laura at all.

Tom thinks of Jim as his best friend, apparently his only friend, at the warehouse. Knowing that Tom often steals time away from his job to write poems, Jim humors Tom, making playful references to him as "Shakespeare." Jim informs him that their supervisor knows about Tom's habit of writing poems on company time. We can assume that Tom knows little about Jim other than that he takes night classes and earns twenty dollars more than he does each month. Tom apparently does not share Jim's outlook on life, and he would never consider attending self-improvement and public-speaking courses. It is his lack of interest in obtaining knowledge about Jim that brings about the sense of desolation at the play's conclusion when Amanda confronts Tom with the truth about Laura's gentleman caller—that he is engaged.

AMANDA: Didn't you call him your best friend down at the warehouse?

TOM: He is, but how did I know?

AMANDA: It seems extremely peculiar that you wouldn't know your best friend was going to be married!

TOM: The warehouse is where I work, not where I know things about people.

AMANDA: You don't know things anywhere!

Tom's ignorance of the truth leads the drama toward the conclusion summarized by a bitter Amanda: "Things have a way of turning out so badly!"

In Amanda's vision Jim is the Wingfields' savior. Laura sees him as a threat to her isolation—a point of view, as we discover, that is well justified. To Tom Jim is a momentary diversion for Amanda and Laura in the waning moments of Tom's role as the breadwinner. The characters therefore relate to Jim according to their illusions. But the Wingfields are not alone in their self-deception. Once he enters the world of the Wingfields, we realize that Jim also is given to illusions of his own.

Through his directions in the text, Williams carefully reveals that Jim's actions onstage betray more than his words; they foreshadow his ultimate betrayal of Laura. From the moment he appears, Jim is a self-absorbed individual who lacks the capacity to involve himself in the lives of others. The playwright's descriptions of Jim throughout the final scene are most revealing. Stripped from the dialogue, the directions present Jim as Williams intended, beginning with their after-dinner conversation:

> (JIM's *attitude is gently humorous. In playing this scene it should be stressed that while the incident is apparently unimportant, it is to* LAURA *the climax of her secret life.*) . . .
>
> (*He extends it* [a glass of dandelion wine] *toward her with extravagant gallantry.*) . . . (*He laughs heartily.* LAURA *takes the glass uncertainly; laughs shyly.*) . . .
>
> (LAURA *returns with the annual. . . . He accepts it reverently. They smile across it with mutual wonder.* LAURA *crouches beside him and they begin to turn through it.* LAURA's *shyness is dissolving in his warmth.*) . . .
>
> (*She gently closes the book in her lap. . . . She hands it* [the operetta program] *to him. He signs it with a flourish*). . . .
>
> (JIM *lights a cigarette and leans indolently back on his elbows smiling at* LAURA *with a warmth and charm which lights her inwardly with altar candles. She remains by the table and turns in her hands a piece of glass to cover her tumult.*) . . .
>
> (*Unconsciously glances at himself in the mirror. . . . He adjusts his tie in the mirror*) . . .
>
> (*His attitude is convincingly dynamic.* LAURA *stares at him, even her shyness is eclipsed in her absolute wonder. He suddenly grins.*) . . .
>
> (*He executes some sweeping turns by himself then holds his arms towards* LAURA.) . . .

(*Suddenly serious. . . . His voice becomes soft and hesitant with a genuine feeling. . . .* LAURA *is abashed beyond speech.*) . . .
(*His voice becomes low and husky.* LAURA *turns away, nearly faint with the novelty of her emotions.*) . . .
(*He suddenly turns her about and kisses her on the lips.*) (*When he releases her,* LAURA *sinks on the sofa with a bright, dazed look*) (JIM *backs away and fishes in his pocket for a cigarette.*) . . . (*He lights the cigarette, avoiding her look.*) . . . (*He coughs decorously and moves a little farther aside as he considers the situation and senses her feelings, dimly, with perturbation.*) . . . (*He pops a mint into his mouth. Then gulps and decides to make a clean breast of it. He speaks slowly and gingerly.*) . . . (LAURA *sways slightly forward and grips the arm of the sofa. He fails to notice, now enrapt in his own comfortable being.*) . . . (*Leaning stiffly forward, clutching the arm of the sofa,* LAURA *struggles visibly with her storm. But* JIM *is oblivious, she is a long way off.*) . . .
(*He crosses deliberately to pick up his hat. The band at the Paradise Dance Hall goes into a tender waltz.*) . . .
(*He stops at the oval mirror to put on his hat. He carefully shapes the brim and the crown to give a discreetly dashing effect.*)

Notice how Jim's gestures throughout the scene indicate his illusory self: "extravagant gallantry," "with a flourish," "convincingly dynamic," "oblivious," and "a discreetly dashing effect." Contrast this with numerous references that reveal that the incident is to Laura the "climax of her secret life." Deftly Williams combines actions with words to achieve this effective characterization. Jim's vision of himself as a man of the promising future is as deceptive as Amanda's vision of herself as a woman from the gallant past.

Should there be any doubt about Jim's superficiality, Tom's narrations dispel them. After informing us of Jim's achievements in high school—"star in basketball, captain of the debating club, president of the senior class and the glee club"—Tom focuses attention on Jim's character. Six years after graduating from high school, Jim has not lived up to his promise. At the age of twenty-three he has a job comparable to Tom's at the warehouse, although Tom is two years younger and has no ambition to advance in his work. Tom is "valuable to him as someone who could remember his former glory" (61). Jim is the kind of person who lives forever on the surface. His "good nature and vitality" are reflections not of his inner life but of his external appearance, which Tom-as-narrator describes as having "the scrubbed and polished look of white chinaware" (61).

Jim is a stranger to the world of Amanda, Laura, and Tom. They receive him, however, because he presents the illusion of escape. Eventually the truth leaks out about Jim: he is no messiah. This man of appearances belongs to a world of mirrors that only reflect one's surface appearance. Even if Jim were not engaged, he could not rescue Laura. His intrusion into her soul is totally unwitting, and his mechanical "Stumble-john" exclamation is his best effort to verbalize his response to an "apparently unimportant" episode in his life.

Tom

As a character Tom is bound by constraints that do not affect him as the narrator. As narrator Tom knows what will happen and has an opinion about the meaning of events onstage. The character, however, awakens each day to the "Rise and Shines" of Amanda, goes to work at a menial job in a shoe warehouse, and spends his evenings writing poems or seeking adventure at the movies. Most who view the play tend to be sympathetic toward Tom. After all he introduces the play and occasionally speaks directly to the audience in the form of soliloquy. However, to appreciate the function of Tom as a character in the play, one must distinguish him from his role as narrator. Williams points out that the narrator in sailor's clothing "takes whatever license with dramatic convention as is convenient to his purposes." He happens to hold vivid memories of four people, one of whom is himself before he left home a number of years earlier.

A familiar argument between Tom and Amanda concerns his

preoccupation with movies. Whenever events at the apartment get on
his nerves, he responds predictably:

AMANDA: But why—*why,* Tom—are you always so *restless?* Where do
          you *go* to, nights?

TOM: I—go to the movies.

AMANDA: Why do you go to the movies so much, Tom?

TOM: I go to the movies because—I like adventure. Adventure is
          something I don't have much of at work, so I go to the
          movies. (scene 4)

Unlike Amanda who is not always conscious of her illusions, Tom
seems fully aware of his. He acknowledges that the movies are a
temporary escape from his boring daily routine at the Continental
Shoemakers. Tom is a would-be poet frustrated by the economic demands placed on him by his mother and sister. He has taken those
demands somewhat seriously and apparently has been the breadwinner for several years. Amanda is counting on him to help provide
for the family until Laura is independent.

Tom copes with boredom by attending movies and writing poems
at home and on the job (when he thinks business is slow and no one
will notice). His deception, Jim tells him, has come to the attention of
their supervisor, Mr. Mendoza. Jim later warns him: "You're going to
be out of a job if you don't wake up." Tom assures him that he is
waking up to "a future that doesn't include the warehouse and Mr.
Mendoza or even a night school course in public speaking" (scene 6).

On one occasion his visit to the movie theater offers him an idea
that proves significant for his life and career. Thanks to a postmovie
appearance by the stage magician named Malvolio, Tom seriously
entertains the notion of escape. He tells Laura about the late night
magic show:

TOM: He performed wonderful tricks, many of them, such as pouring
          water back and forth between pitchers. First it turned to wine
          and then it turned to beer and then it turned to whiskey. I know
          it was whiskey it finally turned into because he needed some-

body to come up out of the audience to help him, and I came up—both shows. . . . But the wonderfullest trick of all was the coffin trick. We nailed him into a coffin and he got out of the coffin without removing one nail. . . . There is a trick that would come in handy for me—get me out of this 2 by 4 situation!

LAURA: Tom—Shhh!

TOM: What're you shushing me for?

LAURA: You'll wake up Mother.

TOM: Goody, goody! Pay'er back for all those "Rise an' Shines. . . . You know it don't take much intelligence to get yourself into a nailed-up coffin, Laura. But who in hell ever got himself out of one without removing one nail?
　　(*As if in answer, the father's grinning photograph lights up.*) (scene 4)

One recalls the playwright's description of Tom in his notes on the characters: "A poet with a job in a warehouse. His nature is not remorseless, but to escape from a trap he has to act without pity." By the end of the fourth scene Tom seems to have moved from his earlier state of frustration to a mood of certainty based on his new-found resolve to leave home.

By the time Jim visits the Wingfields, Tom already has taken steps to extricate himself from his coffinlike existence. Now twenty-one years old, he has modified his previously held view of the movies, as he explains to Jim:

TOM: All the glamorous people—having adventures—hogging it all, gobbling the whole thing up! You know what happens? People go to the movies instead of moving. Hollywood characters are supposed to have all the adventures for everybody in America, while everybody in America sits in a dark room and watches them have them! . . . I'm tired of the movies and I am *about* to *move!*

JIM: Move?

TOM: Yes.

JIM: When?

TOM: Soon!

JIM: Where? Where?

TOM: I'm starting to boil inside. I know I seem dreamy, but inside—well, I'm boiling!—Whenever I pick up a shoe, I shudder a little thinking how short life is and what I am doing! Whatever that means, I know it doesn't mean shoes—except as something to wear on a traveler's feet! (scene 6)

Tom then reveals to Jim a secret he has kept from Amanda: he has joined the Union of Merchant Seamen, having paid his dues with money Amanda had earmarked for the light bill. He shows no remorse, assuming the utility company will not suspend electrical service until after he has left town. He humorously tells Jim he will follow the pattern set by his father, calling himself the "bastard son of a bastard!" (77).

Tom also is following the example of Malvolio the Magician. It was he who gave Tom the idea of gaining effortless escape, the kind of departure Tom believes his father achieved. But Amanda, perhaps unintentionally, makes another connection between the magician and Tom when she tells him at the end of the play: "You live in a dream; you manufacture illusions!" In a few moments, noting that he is preparing to leave the apartment for the movies, she shouts:

> Don't think about us, a mother deserted, an unmarried sister who's crippled and has no job. Don't let anything interfere with your selfish pleasure! Just go, go, go—to the movies . . . Go then! Then go to the moon—you selfish dreamer!

The next time Tom appears he is indeed a dreamer. He also is a magician who, in the words of Amanda, has learned to "manufacture illusions." He greets us with "tricks in his pocket" and gives us "truth in the pleasant disguise of illusion."

CHAPTER 6

An American Memory

Once Laura blows out her candles and Tom finishes his concluding narration, there is little else to say. In words ringing with the eloquence of a poet, Tom says it all. The first response is to applaud the author for providing such an aesthetically pleasing experience. However, after the curtain calls have been made and we leave the imaginary world created by Williams, we may well discover that the play cannot be placed back on the shelf and easily forgotten. There is something about the pantomime of Amanda and Laura, something about the way Tom tells his story, that haunts us. In his closing monologue, Tom confesses that he was "pursued by something. It always came upon me unawares, taking me altogether by surprise." It is the same for many who have experienced the play. Tom so effectively shares his memory with us that we claim it as our own.

We claim the memory because much of it belongs to all who have lived in the twentieth century. Amanda reaches out to us because we recognize in her a sense of tradition that characterizes many reared in distinctive regions. Although her compulsive repetition of stories from her youth may appear foreign to many, her impulse to preserve her single-parent family seems as familiar as the morning newspaper.

Laura and Tom have experienced modern life in typical fashion—in high school or in a temporary job, prodded perhaps by a parent who may be chagrined by offspring who sometimes escape responsibility or who sometimes search wildly for adventure (or both). And who cannot recognize Jim, that "nice, ordinary, young man"?

Since 1945 the play has been performed constantly by community theaters and major companies. Broadway revivals each decade provide directors with new challenges of staging, lighting, and interpretation. Actors and actresses measure their professional achievements by their roles in the play. The play itself has become a litmus test for directors, actors, and critics. When Eddie Dowling played the role of Tom, he charmed the audience with his approachable manner. The audience, with fresh memories of the Great Depression and World War II, readily grasped the references to social events. James Daly's Tom in 1956 was down to earth and factual, allowing Helen Hayes to captivate audiences as Amanda. George Grizzard in 1965 was a calm and understanding Tom. In 1975 Rip Torn departed from tradition and punctuated the narrations with accusing gestures and tones, making many audiences uncomfortable. In 1983 Bruce Davidson, dressed in colorful sweaters played a handsome, blond Tom who was clean-cut and precise.

Each age has its own version of *The Glass Menagerie*. Tom of the 1950s reflects the placid Eisenhower years. In the 1960s it was Tom of the Age of Aquarius whose travels might well carry him eastward. The decade that began with protests over the Vietnam War, the 1970s, brought forth a defiant Tom battling against hypocrisy. In the 1980s Tom seemed more in tune with himself and reminded audiences of conflicts within the American family. The review of the 1983 production by Benedict Nightingale called attention to the relevance of the play to a generation concerned about good parenting:

> Many good mothers have nagged their sons for smoking, and sulked when those sons insulted them, and wept and worried over their daughters, and encouraged and comforted those daughters when life was hurtful. . . . [But her] good intentions . . . make Amanda

dangerous. They camouflage the constant intrusion of "I" and "we" into her conversation; they encourage you to overlook the extent to which her biases are manipulating and shaping an all-adult family; they disguise her unreflecting assumption that what was best for herself is best for her daughter, and what is best for her daughter should dictate her son's behavior.[1]

The play's universal human appeal transcends regions, cultures, and nations. Tom's departure from home is like Mark Twain's Huck Finn who seeks adventure in the West, Herman Melville's Ishmael who goes to sea, Dante who travels into the dark woods, Odysseus who sets his sails toward home. His journey in time—"the longest distance between two places"—is the sort of experience that transcends time. Yet Tom is very much part of a place, just as Huck belongs to the Mississippi and Odysseus to the Mediterranean. Tom's place happens to be St. Louis, Missouri—one of America's "overcrowded urban centers of lower middle-class population." Immediately as the play begins, one discovers how "American" the setting really is.

Instantly we recognize characters who are urged to eat a bowl of Purina for breakfast, who use Durkee's dressing as a condiment with salmon loaf, and who buy butter at Garfinkle's Delicatessen. We know about the mother who carries a "black patent-leather pocketbook with nickel clasps and initials" to the DAR meeting and who sleeps while wearing "metal hair curlers." She is the same woman who comments about fiction by Margaret Mitchell (positive) and D. H. Lawrence (negative), who keeps up with popular fiction about "the horsey set on Long Island" as serialized in the *Home-maker's Companion*.

Laura listens to phonograph records on the wind-up Victrola manufactured by the Radio Corporation of America as she leafs through pages of the *Torch*, the yearbook for Soldan High School. Extracurricular activities there included the debating club, basketball games, and the senior class operetta, *Pirates of Penzance*, by Gilbert and Sullivan. At Soldan High she was enrolled in chorus, which met in the "Aud" (for auditorium) on Mondays, Wednesdays, and Fridays; there she knew a boy nicknamed "Freckles"; there she also encountered the pressure of final exams. Her mother once forced her to attend "the Young People's League at the church." She attended Rubicam's Business College and obtained a typing chart, the Gregg Alphabet. She keeps up with her old classmates by reading the "personal section" of the newspaper.

For a number of years Tom apparently has enjoyed the motion pictures and is quite at home with the names Greta Garbo, Clark Gable, and Mickey Mouse. The silver screen also provides trips abroad courtesy of the travelogue and the latest world events via the newsreel. The ceilings of the modern warehouse where he works are made of "celotex," and lighting is by fluorescent tubes. He incorporates references to the underworld for dramatic effect—"the Hogan gang," "tommy gun," "cat houses," "opium dens," "czar of the underworld," and "gambling casinos." He reads a daily newspaper, the *St. Louis Post Dispatch*. Tom smokes cigarettes—a "pack a day at fifteen cents a pack." He has made plans to join the merchant marines and pays his dues with money intended for the light bill.

Jim is a high school hero who won the silver cup in debate, sang the lead in the senior class operetta, starred in basketball, and served as "president of the senior class and the glee club." Does his future include nothing short of the White House? Toward that end, perhaps, he has enrolled in a night course in public speaking where he has learned about the importance of having social poise and of not having an inferiority complex. During the summer of 1934, Jim was indelibly impressed with the exhibits of science and industry at the Century of Progress world fair that marked the centennial of Chicago; he also waxes enthusiastically about the genius named Wrigley who made a fortune in chewing gum and who built an impressive skyscraper. Jim also has a keen interest in electrodynamics, the future of television, and radio engineering. If he has a favorite part of the newspaper, it is the sports section, and he knows about the activities of the colorful pitcher for the St. Louis Cardinals, Dizzy Dean. In his coat pocket he carries, in addition to gum, a roll of peppermint Life Savers. His vocabulary includes slang expresions: "Holy Jeez," "a helluva lot," "you drip," "I'll be jiggered," and "Stumble-john."

An American Memory

The world in which the characters live, move, and breathe is unmistakably that of the United States of the 1930s. In drama such verisimilitude lends the aura of authenticity, and in this regard Williams is paying his respects to Chekhov and the realists. Of more importance, however, is that Williams's plethora of Americana serves a larger purpose, one that readers and critics often overlook. This drama depicting the Wingfield family's moment of crisis is analogous to a larger drama being played out on the stage of American history.

While the characters are at home in the popular culture of America during the 1930s, they also embody traditions and trends that help make the analogy work. We can better understand the characters by placing them in the context of David Riesman's classic study of the American character, *The Lonely Crowd*. Most Americans have been influenced by two basic approaches to life: inner direction and other direction, Riesman explains. The inner-directed Amanda lives with a system of values implanted by her parents and authority figures of her community, and she gains a sense of meaning when she conducts her life according to these values. Amanda lives as though a gyroscope had been implanted in her being, and she may be temporarily disoriented by life; however, her "automatic pilot" returns her to her original upright position established by her traditional culture. Jim splendidly represents Riesman's other-directed man who operates as though he were controlled by radar, constantly sending out signals and adjusting his movement to conform to his environment. Riesman finds that this type of individual characterizes especially the American middle class for much of the twentieth century: "shallower, freer with his money, friendlier, more uncertain of himself and his values, more demanding of approval."[2] Clearly this is the world in which Jim O'Connor aspires to live, and his radar seems to be in working order.

The twenty-one-year-old Tom rejects both Amanda's and Jim's approaches to life in favor of engaging in a quest for adventure that may lead him to find what he knows has been "lost." He generally fits the "new" type of personality Riesman sees on the horizon, the autonomous man. Tom appears to be on the road toward autonomy from the very beginning. He obtains sustenance from the inner-directed pattern of existence. He has an internal guidance system, a gyroscope, and he does not constantly adjust his behavior to fit the expectations of his known and unknown peers. He humors Amanda but does not share her worldview. He has his library, as it were, and Amanda has hers. Many of the titles of books on his shelf seem foreign to his mother whose literary tastes probably are defined by the *Home-maker's Companion.*

Just because Tom rejects much of his mother's view of the world does not mean that he has abandoned tradition. Rather he has allied himself with a connection to the past that is called the literary tradition, represented in part by the British novelist D. H. Lawrence. There are other authors, of course, surely including the real Shakespeare behind his nickname at the warehouse. Tom seems to find in his own life a sense of significance that allows him to meet the world with a degree of confidence. Although a loner, Tom is comfortable with himself and with his ambition to become a poet. All he needs is the maturity and the occasion to bring it all to pass.

Jim, on the other hand, acts on impulses derived from his courses in public speaking and night classes on technological subjects. His eyes light up when Amanda speaks entertainingly. But Jim is oblivious to the past. He is unaware of ideas that have motivated men and women in history, save those he might have picked up through illustrations in his public speaking course. If Tom's approach to life is determined in great measure by his ambition to contribute to the literary tradition, then Jim's approach is determined by his ambition to gain power through social poise. Jim prefigures the organizational man of the 1950s and beyond, about whom sociologists have written a great deal. The basic difference between the two young men is that Tom relates to the world as an independent agent, whereas Jim is totally dependent on the approval of others.

As narrator, Tom's mission in life is to help us better understand these two distinctive representations of the American character. Amanda, "clinging frantically to another time and place," reflects in part the nation's past. Jim, with "starry" eyes, holds a vision of its future. They symbolically embody options not only for Laura but for the future of a world "lit by lightning."

Amanda's myth of the South is one she absorbed as a young woman reared in the Mississippi Delta. She also had other sources of values. The Protestant Episcopal church gave her a thorough acquaintance with holy scripture, as is evident in her conversation. Her genealogical tree is rooted deeply in American history, and members of the St. Louis chapter of the Daughters of the American Revolution elected her to office.

The South of Amanda's youth was a land of ritual. The gentlemen callers she refers to so often were part of an ordered existence. There she learned the art of conversation and discussed with young men "things of importance in the world! Never anything coarse or common or vulgar" (9). While helping Laura prepare for her gentleman caller, Amanda says, "All pretty girls are a trap, a pretty trap, and men expect them to be" (64). The trap involves more than physical beauty. Although Amanda says she was not slighted in terms of "a pretty face and a graceful figure," she learned early the importance of having a "nimble wit and a tongue to meet all occasions" (9).

Amanda's plight might be interpreted as an indictment of the southern system of values she inherited. The system allowed her to meet and marry a handsome and charming young gentleman, only to have him desert her when Laura was eight and Tom was six years old. Amanda acknowledges that she "wasn't prepared for what the future brought me" (80). However, she never questions the pattern of her youth, assuming only that she made a mistake when she married Mr. Wingfield. That she faithfully seeks to pass down the courtship ritual to Laura is a commentary on the strength and vitality of the tradition the inner-directed Amanda inherited.

Williams depicts Amanda as a darker image of Scarlett O'Hara, heroine of Margaret Mitchell's epic novel, *Gone with the Wind*. The play's references to the best-selling novel provide the playwright with a point of reference. Scarlett, an antebellum belle who moves up in the world, eventually faces crushing defeat at the hands of the enemy of the "Southern way of life." Amanda's description of herself as a young woman in Blue Mountain could allow her to pass for Scarlett—"a pretty face and a graceful figure," possessing a "nimble wit."

When the lights go out on Scarlett and her way of life, she heroically digs in her feet and plans to regain her position "tomorrow." (Scarlett's resolve is said to have galvanized an entire generation of southerners.) At the end of *The Glass Menagerie,* however, there is nothing in Amanda resembling the stubborn resolution of the heroine of Tara. On a set lighted by a warped candelabrum rescued from a fire that long ago burned her beloved Episcopal church, Amanda has nothing to say as she comforts her daughter. Amanda has said it all already, and the words have proved useless. As Laura blows out the candles, we sense Williams's ironic observation about the relevance of the southern tradition, at least one version of it, to a generation of Americans "matriculating in a school for the blind" (5).

Amanda's option for Laura's future contrasts sharply with that provided by Jim, the gentleman caller. This "nice, ordinary young man" is a carefully drawn portrait of the upwardly mobile male so highly regarded by American society, particularly by the business community, in the twentieth century. Jim brings to bear an All-American background: a leader of his class, a hero in athletics, a star in the senior operetta, and a champion debater. His very aspect is forward looking: "always running or bounding, never just walking" (61), as Tom describes him.

Jim is a devoted student of the science of self-improvement. His night course in public speaking is especially appropriate. Perhaps he attends one that the Dale Carnegie organization has been offering since the 1920s for business and professional men. Jim's attitude perfectly matches Carnegie's view of the ideal man, as outlined in *How to Win Friends and Influence People,* a best-seller since 1936: "the man who has technical knowledge *plus* the ability to express his ideas, to assume leadership, and to arouse enthusiasm among men—that man is headed for higher earning power."[3] Carnegie's famous course combines public speaking with related topics, such as salesmanship, human relations, and applied psychology.

Jim embodies much of Carnegie's description of a man with a future. He has technical knowledge, and it happens to be in the area of media—radio engineering and television. Even Laura momentarily is entranced by the enthusiasm with which Jim describes his personal plans for his future in television:

> I wish to be ready to go up right along with it. Therefore I'm planning to get in on the ground floor. In fact I've already made the right connections and all that remains is for the industry itself to get under way! (scene 7)

That he has an ability to express his ideas is obvious. He conducts himself with the positive self-assurance of an effective salesman who, when he fails to make a deal, knows the difference between being "disappointed" and "discouraged."

He has taken seriously other aspects of the Carnegie-type course as well. Jim gets along well with people and has gained the confidence of his boss, Mr. Mendoza. He also has a working knowledge of "applied psychology," as he explains to Laura:

> I have a friend who says I can analyze people better than doctors that make a profession of it. I don't claim that to be necessarily true, but I can sure guess a person's psychology, Laura! . . . Yep—that's what I judge to be your principal trouble. A lack of confidence in yourself as a person. You don't have the proper amount of faith in yourself.

Jim provides a name for Laura's problem: "inferiority complex." Then he summarizes Laura's real need: "You know what my strong advice to you is? Think of yourself as *superior* in some way!" (103). He says his superiority is in the technical area of "electrodynamics," and he asserts that Laura surely can cultivate something. The conversation then focuses not on Laura but on Jim who, according to stage directions, "unconsciously glances at himself in the mirror" before describing his night course in public speaking. Jim applies his psychology to Laura long enough only to give her condition a clinical-sounding name—inferiority complex.

Although Jim symbolically and literally sweeps Laura off her feet, for a few moments at least, he does not unduly impress the friend from the warehouse he calls "Shakespeare." Tom undoubtedly knows little about Jim's personal life, as he explains to Amanda near the end of the play. But obviously he has made up his mind that Jim's views about success are superficial. Jim seems to confirm Tom's judgment again and again, beginning with his glib comment upon shaking the cold hand of a timid Laura, "You ought to play a little hot swing music to warm you up" (72). As Tom and Jim await the serving of dinner, Tom picks up the *Post Dispatch* and assumes he knows the section Jim would like to read: "The comics?" Tom is wrong, of course, because Jim asks for "Sports!" and glances at it briefly.

When Jim tries to encourage Tom to take a night class in public speaking, Jim unconsciously undercuts his efforts by saying "Shakespeare—I'm going to sell you a bill of goods!" (73). As Tom sees it, propaganda for a night class in public speaking is indeed "a bill of goods"—a false promise, a hoax. Perhaps Jim's most telling self-indictment occurs while the screen projection reveals the image of an an executive at his desk:

JIM: It fits you for—executive positions!

TOM: Awww.

JIM: I tell you it's done a helluva lot for me.

TOM: In what respect?

JIM: In every! Ask yourself what is the difference between you an' me and men in the office down front? Brains?—No!—Ability?—No! Then what? Just one little thing—

TOM: What is that one little thing?

JIM: Primarily it amounts to—social poise! Being able to square up to people and hold your own on any social level!

Jim does not recognize that underlying his exposition about social poise is a cynical view of success in America. His position is built on a crass and flimsy assumption that a person does not need to develop the mind in order to reach the top of one's job or profession; one does not even need any distinctive ability. The key is to act as though one already is successful. This seems to be what Jim means when he talks about the primary importance of social poise. In Tom's view it is a "little thing" indeed.

At the beginning of the play, Tom's narration prepares us to view Jim as a character of symbolic importance. He is "an emissary from a world of reality that we were somehow set apart from." He also represents the hope that an outsider, a kind of messiah, will rescue the Wingfields. Jim is "the long delayed but always expected something that we live for." But Jim does not fulfill his messianic mission. He remains a stranger to the world of Amanda, Laura, and Tom. They receive him, however, because he presents the illusion of escape. Instead of saving the Wingfields, Jim precipitates their collapse. At the end what endures is Tom's memory of the abiding quality of human love represented in the pantomime of Amanda and Laura in candlelight.

Jim's failure to help the Wingfields find a solution to their problem is significant in view of the social background of the play provided by Tom's opening narration. Set in "that quaint period, the thirties," the play's events occur when America's middle class faced personal and social crises created by economic collapse. The set for scene 1 is described as an apartment in "one of those vast hive-like conglomerations of cellular living units that flower as warty growths in overcrowded urban centers." The Wingfields live among the lower middle class, which the stage directions for scene 1 describe as the "largest and fundamentally enslaved section of American society." The entrance to their apartment is a fire-escape—a name with "a touch of accidental poetic truth, for all of these huge buildings are always burning with the slow and implacable fires of human desperation."

He describes the times of the Great Depression as a painful moment "when the huge middle class of America was matriculating in a school for the blind." Tom finds it ironic that the condition fundamentally was self-induced: "Their eyes had failed them, or they had failed their eyes, and so they were having their fingers pressed forcibly down on the fiery Braille alphabet of a dissolving economy" (5). They also were blind to the significance of the political rumblings from the European continent in the 1930s. Even in the United States there were clear indications of disorder, such as those "disturbances of labor, sometimes pretty violent, in otherwise peaceful cities such as Chicago, Cleveland, Saint Louis." But the population, bent on pursuing deceptions, could not grasp the meaning of such events. As though distracted by the rhythmical music of its nightclubs and bars, America seemed caught up in a frenzied dance on the edge of its grave. In the world, however, the sobering reality of war had awakened the consciences of many. In his opening monologue Tom recalls: "In Spain there was revolution. Here there was only shouting and confusion."

Tom believes that America soon will become a nation at war. The newspaper in the Wingfields' apartment carries daily reports of the revolution in Spain. (The headline "Franco Triumphs!" could refer to any number of victories by the Spanish nationalist army against Spain's government between October 1936 and March 1939, when the army, led by General Francisco Franco, captured Madrid and established a dictatorship, supported by Spain's fascist political party, the Falange Española.) At the beginning of scene 5, the narrator's words can be read as a poem of lament. Images of "brief, deceptive rainbows" contrast with the flashing terror of "bombardments."

The poetic narration also contains a reference to world history that should not go unnoticed:

> Suspended in the mist over Berchtesgaden, caught in the folds of Chamberlain's umbrella—

The allusion to the mist has to do with Adolf Hitler's private retreat, the Eagle's Nest, located on the peak of the mountain Obersalzberg, some 1,640 feet above Berchtesgaden in southeastern Germany. Herman Göring, Martin Bormann, and other Nazi leaders had residences there, along with air raid shelters and barracks. Without Neville Chamberlain, Hitler could not have achieved so easily his position of power. Williams employs the popular image of the British prime minister who typically was photographed umbrella in hand. At the Munich Conference in 1938, Chamberlain signed an agreement with Adolf Hitler and Benito Mussolini sanctioning Germany's acquisition of Sudetenland, formerly part of Czechoslovakia. In fact Chamberlain's agreement merely encouraged Hitler's lust for European real estate, a lust that eventually led to the war. Therefore those who compensate for "change or adventure" by frequenting the Paradise Dance Hall, like the rest of the world, will be "caught in the folds" of world events not of their own making:

> In Spain there was Guernica!
> But here there was only hot swing music and liquor, dance halls, bars, movies, and sex that hung in the gloom like a chandelier and flooded the world with brief, deceptive rainbows. . . .
> All the world was waiting for bombardments!

Tom sardonically tells Jim in scene 6 that Americans prefer "*movies*" over "*moving.*" Then he prophetically alludes to the impending conflict:

> Hollywood characters are supposed to have all the adventures for everybody in America, while everybody in America sits in a dark room and watches them have them! Yes, until there's a war. That's when adventure becomes available to the masses.

The tendency of Americans to ignore the meaning of world events is made vivid by the popular, success-oriented Jim O'Connor who glances occasionally at the sports section while ignoring the newspaper's headlines about Franco's revolution and Hitler's storm troopers. When Tom concludes the play, we realize the cumulative effect of the many references to social conditions and worldwide political unrest. It is not that America is a sleeping giant, soon to spring forth from its slumber. Rather its citizens have failed their eyes, complacently opting for the security of self-deception. The nation's appointment with destiny is at hand, Tom says, and soon everyone will discover that "the world is lit by lightning."

Many editions of *The Glass Menagerie* contain as a preface an essay Williams wrote after the play became a household name. Entitled "The Catastrophe of Success," it concludes with a commentary that provides insight into his concept of the social responsibility of an artist:

> Then what is good? The obsessive interest in human affairs, plus a certain amount of compassion and moral conviction, that first made the experience of living something that must be translated into pigment or music or bodily movement or poetry or prose or anything that's dynamic and expressive—that's what's good for you if you're at all serious in your aims. William Saroyan wrote a great play on this theme, that purity of heart is the one success worth having. "In the time of your life—live!" That time is short and it doesn't return again. It is slipping away while I write this and while you read it, and the monosyllable of the clock is Loss, loss, loss, unless you devote your heart to its opposition.

The Glass Menagerie is more than Williams's private glimpse into the lives of the Wingfields. It is also a memory of America during a critical period of history, the Great Depression. The play is firmly rooted in the fertile soil of the intellectual and political history of the twentieth century. The playwright deliberately incorporates popular culture, social trends, and historical developments appropriate for the circumstances of the period. To read the play merely as Tom's subjective memory of his family is to overlook a fairly obvious effort by Williams to create a memory of a truly contemporary time and place.

CHAPTER 7

The Voyager's Quest

TOM: I'm planning to change. (*He leans over the rail speaking with quiet exhilaration. The incandescent marquees and signs of the first-run movie houses light his face from across the alley. He looks like a voyager.*)

Why does Tom leave home? This basic question about *The Glass Menagerie* is one we seldom ask because the answer seems so obvious: he leaves because his mother eventually drives him away by yelling, "Go to the moon," just once too often—the same sort of rationale that likely motivated his father some sixteen years earlier. Taking seriously hints in the text, we might gather that he leaves because he joins the merchant marines. Satisfactory as both these answers appear to be, one should recall that he does not leave St. Louis until he is forced to leave. He loses his job at the shoe warehouse after the evening he brought Jim home. "I was fired for writing a poem on the lid of a shoe-box," Tom explains in the closing narration. (The narrator's clothing suggests that he is now a sailor.) Had Tom not been fired, how long would he have continued to live at home, "burning with the slow and implacable fires of human desperation?" The question is hypothetical, but the point is that the drama allows us to raise such a question.

There is much at home that Tom finds infuriating. His mother constantly corrects him, urging him to "masticate" his food, to sit up straight, to eat a good breakfast, to let his coffee cool before drinking it, to wear his muffler, to comb his hair, to quit smoking cigarettes, to avoid drunkenness, to stop going to the movies so often, and so on. On the intellectual level, Amanda, who views D. H. Lawrence as "insane," seems totally out of touch with the kind of contemporary literature Tom enjoys.

Tom also has grown weary of her repertoire of tales from Blue Mountain, and when he senses she is about to repeat her familiar cycle, he immediately protests. Even so, prompted by his sister, he allows her the privilege and even encourages her from time to time: "How did you entertain those gentleman callers?" he askes in scene 1. Knowing almost by heart the words that will follow, he enters into her conversation with an ironic humor that goes unnoticed by his mother. Indeed Tom seems to derive no little pleasure from the repartee.

At times, however, Amanda pushes Tom over the edge, and he retaliates with fierce words and angry gestures. In scene 2, precipitated by her objection to his nightly visits to the movies, Tom and his mother engage in a fierce argument that ends with her crying: "I won't speak to you—until you apologize!" This particular argument is worth noticing because two crucial issues emerge. First, we realize how deeply demeaning Tom believes his work to be:

> Listen! You think I'm crazy *about* the *warehouse?* (*He bends fiercely toward her slight figure*) You think I'm in love with the Continental Shoemakers? You think I want to spend fifty-five *years* down there in that—*celotex interior!* with *fluorescent—tubes!* Look! I'd rather somebody picked up a crowbar and battered out my brains—than go back mornings! I *go!* Everytime you come in yelling that God damn *"Rise and Shine!" "Rise and Shine!"* I say to myself, "How *lucky dead* people are!" But I get up. I *go!* For sixty-five dollars a month I give up all that I dream of doing and being *ever!* And you say self—*self's* all I ever think of. Why, listen, if self is

what I thought of, Mother, I'd be where he is—GONE! (*Pointing to
father's picture*) As far as the system of transportation reaches!
(scene 2)

The second insight revealed in their argument concerns his image
of himself. He does not regard himself as a self-preoccupied artist. We
know that Tom dreams of being a writer because he spends his free
time either writing or going to the movies. At this stage in his life, the
image of the poet as adventurer, like Hart Crane's young poet in his
"Voyagers" poems, is a very appealing role model. The job at the
Continental Shoemakers prevents him from doing what he would like
to do. Why, then, does he keep going back each day, goaded by his
mother's early-morning "Rise and Shine"? He says he does not go for
himself. He rejects the notion that he is selfish. He fully understands
the meaning of self-oriented behavior. For sixteen years he has been
looking at an image of this kind of behavior each day in that smiling
likeness that ironically decorates the Wingfields' apartment.

Tom goes to work each day because he knows he is responsible for
the welfare of his mother and sister. He is the only stable source of
income for this single-parent family. He lives with his mother and
older sister, and he seems to have a sense of familial attachment.
Amanda perhaps recognizes all this. At times she reveals keen insight
into her son's character. After he apologizes to her in scene 4, she
assumes some of the blame for the argument. She understandingly
accepts his pattern of strange behavior because she realizes that his
"ambitions do not lie in the warehouse." However, she says she cannot understand his constant need for adventure. Thus when he leaves
the apartment for another night at the movies at the end of the play,
Amanda again accuses him of putting himself above the welfare of
Laura and herself:

AMANDA: Go to the movies, go! Don't think about us, a mother de-
          serted, an unmarried sister who's crippled and has no job!
          Don't let anything interfere with your selfish pleasure! Just
          go, go, go—to the movies!

TOM: All right, I will! The more you shout about my selfishness to me the quicker I'll go, and I won't go to the movies!

AMANDA: Go, then! Then go to the moon—you selfish dreamer! (TOM *smashes his glass on the floor. He plunges out on the fire-escape, slamming the door.* LAURA *screams—cut by door.*)

Shortly after his dramatic departure from the apartment, as he recalls, he was fired and then began his travels throughout the world. Does this action imply that he selfishly left Amanda and Laura alone and defenseless for the sake of self-discovery? For that reason alone? Is he really emulating his "bastard" father? Or is he, to use his own words, exercising his will by beginning his quest "to find in motion what was lost in space"?

Tom has contemplated leaving home for some time, and Amanda is well aware of his correspondence with the merchant marine. Tom can talk convincingly about the need to gain independence, especially as he shows signs of maturation at the end of the play. He tells Jim in scene 6 that he has become "tired of the movies." He wants to have his own adventures rather than to continue to live vicariously through Clark Gable:

> I'm starting to boil inside. I know I seem dreamy, but inside—well, I'm boiling!—whenever I pick up a shoe, I shudder a little thinking how short life is and what I am doing—whatever that means, I know it doesn't mean shoes—except as something to wear on a traveler's feet!

However sincere his sentiments are, the fact remains that he returns again and again to his stifling job at the shoe warehouse until he is forced to leave. Tom's reluctance to cut the apron strings that bind him is significant, for he has reasons not to make the break. The playwright's character description suggests that "to escape from a trap he has to act without pity." This aptly describes Tom as we first see him, for he obviously has escaped. However, another part of the description that appropriately describes Tom is as follows: "His nature is not remorseless." Having meditated a lifetime on the meaning of the doughboy's smile, he knows well both the impulse to abandon and the consequences of abandonment.

Tom belongs to that generation of Americans he indicts in the narrations and soliloquies. It seems that he too is the kind of person who must be acted upon before he will act. Perhaps he is describing himself when he speaks of those patrons of the Paradise Dance Hall who are mesmerized by the "delicate rainbow colors" reflected by the slowly turning glass ball suspended from the ceiling. It takes an external event to awaken him to action.

Tom's fate is to become a fugitive poet. His quest is "to find in motion what was lost in space." (123). What he finds, after leaving St. Louis, is a lot of other cities that on the surface appear enticing, but the bright color reminds him of leaves "torn away from the branches," perhaps by the cold winds of autumn. The image is fitting for the world also, where sunshine has been replaced by lightning. Traveling alone is no solace for Tom, because he forever remembers a particular moment in his past: "I pass the lighted window of a shop where perfume is sold. The window is filled with pieces of colored glass, tiny transparent bottles in delicate colors, like bits of a shattered rainbow" (124).

Tom's burden is the memory of his past. His previous narrations suggest he may be making a broad reference at this point. Many Americans chased "brief, deceptive rainbows" in the 1930s. That was while "the world was waiting for bombardments!" In the war these "kids" finally get their share of "adventure and change." We also can interpret Tom's "shattered rainbow" as a more narrowly focused reference to the Wingfield family. As Tom speaks, we see Amanda, described as having *"dignity and tragic beauty"* comfort her daughter. The poet Tom relates this image in the perfume shop window to Laura's broken dreams, her unfulfilled life.

At this point we can understand better the meaning of the epigraph to *The Glass Menagerie:* "Nobody, not even the rain, has such small hands." Few readers notice the line, and fewer still consider its relationship to the drama. But Williams selected it for reasons he considered important. (Indeed, most of his plays have epigraphs that provide insights into his interpretation of his work.) For this play he chose the concluding line of E. E. Cummings's poem, "somewhere i have never travelled." The imagery of the poem is the flower bud as it awaits the gentle hands of the spring breeze to unfold its petals and turn it into a full blossom. It is an image for the world of the play, because the characters, like everyone else, seem to be waiting for external events to awaken them into action. Once Tom loses his job, we gather that he blossoms to the extent that he leaves home and begins his life as a poet.

The haunting aspect of the epigraph concerns Laura. We recall that the shy sister of Tom often visits the house of tropical flowers, "the jewel box," during her walks in the park. On the warm spring evening that Jim O'Connor visits the Wingfields, the rains are just beginning to fall as he arrives. For a few moments she appears to be ready to open her petals until Jim betrays her hopes. Then we see on Laura's face "a look of almost infinite desolation." As Laura says, "Blue is wrong for roses." Her petals are not the kind that will open.

Will Laura complete her life without experiencing the gentle awakening symbolized by the warm spring rains of the human spirit? Such a fate is possible for her, if not probable. The thought particularly disturbs her younger brother. Tom also is concerned about his mother's future and, in a more general way, the future of all those souls in America "burning with the slow and implacable fires of human desperation" (3). These are the memories that Tom must bear as he travels throughout the world. It is a burden, however, that a few chosen individuals like Tom must bear. Tom happens to be among those very few whose perception of life becomes a work of art. Although the cost of remembering is high, it is the price every true artist must pay. It is the unnegotiable price Tom especially must pay as he creates his enduring masterpiece. Writing a poem on the lid of a shoe box was his first step.

Earlier we considered hypothetically the question of whether Tom would have left home had not his boss fired him. The purpose of the question is to focus attention on the deep attachment Tom feels for his mother and sister. His profound concern for them also is an analogy for his attachment to the people of America whose lives reflect the nation's expectations for an awakening (thus the popular song played at the Paradise Dance Hall, "All The World Is Waiting for the Sunrise"). Citizens began the 1930s in the gloom of an expanding economic depression. Many tried to ignore reality only to have their "fingers pressed forcibly down on the fiery Braille alphabet." The Wingfields therefore are both victims and representatives of a dark chapter in the social history of America.

As the spectacle of the Wingfields unfolds onstage, Williams reminds us of a larger political crisis that will force America to take action. The deceptions that motivated Chamberlain at the Munich Conference, whether innocent or self-willed, inevitably will affect each person who lives in the free world. Within the low hanging clouds above the beautiful German town of Berchtesgaden, the leaders of the Third Reich plot moves that will catapult the world into the chaos of war. The United States, chasing "brief, deceptive rainbows," seems unable to penetrate the mist of Adolf Hitler's schemes. Attuned to the spirit of the 1930s, the poet Tom senses the impending crisis. Yet the character Tom lives in suspension like other members of his generation, awaiting the inevitable.

Although Tom has planned to move for some time, he has trouble taking that first painful step. Memories of home, both sweet and bittersweet, bind him. Once he loses his job, Tom fuses his instincts with action. He becomes in fact what he had been in his imagination for some time: the young man as artist. His first great work of the imagination, however, is not about his life as a voyager. He creates a penetrating vision of truth disguised as art. Tom sensitively recovers the meaning of those events that molded him into an artist. The act, indeed, is a kind of inverted magic, for he presents the truth about himself—the master of illusion.

As an artist Tom travels in a world of cities and people who appear to have been cut loose from their moorings. These separated parts belong together. Leaves belong to limbs, and limbs belong to trees, and trees belong to roots that go deep into the earth. Seeking to find "in motion what was lost in space," Tom makes the discovery that these images of impermanence remind him so much of himself.

Tom says he "was pursued by something. It always came upon me unawares, taking me altogether by surprise" (124). The vision of Amanda and Laura always is the same, "like bits of a shattered rainbow." Tom remembers them only to incorporate with their memory other realities of the American nation in the 1930s. When he translates that larger memory into the perfect disguise of illusion, he creates a masterpiece of the imagination we know as *The Glass Menagerie.* Certainly it is a good thing that Tom finally leaves home. He becomes a voyager through some of the crucial decades of the twentieth century. Tom becomes the poet of the American memory.

CHAPTER 8

Tradition and Technique

The curtain rises and reveals the depressing wall of a tenement building, framed by a jagged network of fire escapes, clothes lines, and garbage cans. As the narrator concludes his introduction, a transparency allows the wall to reveal the inside of the Wingfields' apartment. The audience observes the beginning of the first scene through the wall as it slowly ascends out of view. The characters are seated for a meal, and they use gestures required for eating, but there is no food on the table, nor are there utensils. The text calls for the projection of a line from a fifteenth-century French ballad on a screen as we hear a mother call her son to the dinner table. Thus begins *The Glass Menagerie*.

The unusual setting surprises audiences today, perhaps, as much as it did those of the 1940s. A British reviewer wrote that the play was a "patchwork bubble of sentimental imagining"; he said the characters were less than real and that Amanda and Laura in the final scene "appear like dim specimens in some pixyologist's elfarium."[1] More than likely the reviewer was taken aback by the pervading sense of unreality Williams incorporated into his "memory play." Although the vast majority of critics and audiences have not found the play to be "sentimental imagining," the reviewer raised a good question: How can a nonrealistic play present an audience with a vision of real people? The question leads directly to the nature of Williams's contribution to the modern stage.

Two concepts pertinent for discussions of twentieth-century drama appear prominently in the author's prefatory production notes for *The Glass Menagerie:* expressionism and realism. Williams identifies with the former and rejects the latter. He claims that expressionism offers the following advantages:

> Expressionism and all other unconventional techniques in drama have only one valid aim, and that is a closer approach to truth. When a play employs unconventional techniques, it is not, or certainly shouldn't be, trying to escape its responsibility of dealing with reality, or interpreting experience, but is actually or should be attempting to find a closer approach, a more penetrating and vivid expression of things as they are.

He considered the achievements of the realists to be significant, and he often mentioned his debt to Chekhov, whose earlier works especially were in the realistic tradition. (A letter written to Donald Windham while he was working an early version of *The Glass Menagerie* reveals that Williams's study wall contained a "nicely framed" picture of Chekhov.)[2] However, at the beginning of his career, he sensed the need to move beyond realism:

> The straight realistic play with its genuine frigidaire and authentic ice-cubes, its characters that speak exactly as its audience speaks, corresponds to the academic landscape and has the same virtue of a photographic likeness. Everyone should know nowadays the unimportance of the photographic in art: that truth, life, or reality is an organic thing which the poetic imagination can represent or suggest, in essence, only through transformation, through changing into other forms than those which were merely present in appearance.
>
> These remarks are not meant as a preface only to this particular play. They have to do with a conception of a new, plastic theatre that must take the place of the exhausted theatre of realistic conventions if the theatre is to resume vitality as a part of our culture.

Williams probably was not deliberately aligning himself with the Bauhaus school of the expressionist theoreticians Walter Gropius, Wassily Kandinsky, and Paul Klee. Neither was he indicating a preference for certain plays, such as Luigi Pirandello's *Six Characters in Search of an Author* or Jean Cocteau's *The Infernal Machine*. Rather the concept of expressionism gave him the latitude that permitted him to bring into the theater a variety of nontheatrical approaches, such as poetic dialogue, theme and background music, impressionistic lighting, and transparent stage settings. Without these elements we could never enter so deeply into the world of Tom's memory.

If Williams borrowed from the tradition of realism, as modified by the expressionists, he also borrowed from an art form with distinctively American associations: the cinema. During the 1920s and 1930s the young Williams resembled Tom. He spent a great deal of his spare time in movie houses, watching silent films, which typically were accompanied by a piano or a small orchestra. In the absence of dialogue, movie directors depended on carefully placed titles. If movies are imitations of the drama—a single performance frozen in time—then Williams decided to see whether drama might benefit from some of the techniques movie directors used. An immediate example of this borrowing is the large picture of the smiling doughboy, the absent Mr. Wingfield. In this case most directors follow the playwright's suggestion that it light up at precisely the right moment near the beginning of scene 4 when an inebriated Tom tells Laura about the "escape" of Malvolio the Magician.

In traditional theater the floodlight follows the action, illuminating the characters engaged in dialogue. In the view of Williams, however, there is another kind of dramatic action which often takes place in a location apart from the dialogue. The third scene begins with a narration by Tom, followed by Amanda's solicitation of a magazine order over the telephone. That is all that happens before the stage dims. Momentarily the lights return, and we hear the beginning of an argument between Tom and Amanda. But what we see is the frail figure of Laura, *"with clenched hands and panicky expression."* Williams calls for a *"clear pool of light on her figure throughout this scene.*" Meanwhile Tom and Amanda engage in a fierce verbal battle *"behind the portieres,"* jointly firing a total of nineteen exchanges. Once Tom and Amanda appear, *"the upstage area is lit with a turgid smoky red glow."* This confrontation between Tom and Amanda is a turning point in the drama because it leads eventually to a mutual apology and to Amanda's request that Tom fetch a gentleman caller for Laura. Yet the real action takes place elsewhere. By focusing the *"clear pool of light"* on Laura, Williams suggests that the barbs so brutally exchanged between Tom and Amanda find their mark deep inside Laura.

The production notes speak of the need for "a new, plastic theatre," suggesting possibilities previously explored only by the motion picture. The appearance of cinematic techniques in *The Glass Menagerie* is a major development in the drama, a development that may be related to the circumstances under which he began to write the play. Williams was not only drawing on his early fascination with motion pictures. His agent, Audrey Wood, had helped him obtain a job as a screenwriter for Metro Goldwyn Mayer in 1943. He was supposed to write a screenplay as a vehicle for the actress Lana Turner, but he quickly realized that he could not put his heart into it. Independently he prepared some original film outlines and proposals for M-G-M. He immersed himself in the techniques of a medium he had admired from a distance as a youth. One screenplay about which he felt strongly was based on his short story, "Portrait of a Girl in Glass." He gave it the title "The Gentleman Caller." Already he had decided upon the actress to play the role of Laura, and his hopes were high. However, M-G-M turned down the proposal almost immediately. Williams later recalled an executive's rationale: *Gone with the Wind* had sufficiently treated the subject of southern women. (After *The Glass Menagerie* had achieved commercial and critical success, M-G-M engaged in a losing battle with Warner Brothers Studios to purchase film rights to the play.)

A continuing debate among students of Williams and the drama is the matter of those movielike projections that appear forty-four times. Most directors have eliminated the projections completely, focusing attention more directly on the delicate interaction among the four characters. When he prepared the text for reading, however, Williams insisted that the projections be included. His production notes suggest that they offer "a definite emotional appeal." Then he gives directors an unusual invitation to "invent many other uses for this device than those indicated in the present script."

From an "architectural" standpoint, he believed the images and legends would help audiences better grasp the narrative line. "Each scene contains a particular point (or several) which is structurally the most important." The reader might test Williams's theory by engaging in a brief exercise in mental association. The object is to recall quickly memories of exact moments in the drama prompted by the following list of ten images and ten quotations that appear on the screen:

Images

Amanda as a girl on a porch, greeting callers
a swarm of typewriters
Jim as a high school hero bearing a silver cup
glamor magazine cover
sailing vessel with Jolly Roger
caller with bouquet
moon
Amanda as a girl
executive at desk
Blue Roses image

Quotations

"Ou sont les neiges"
"After the fiasco"
"You think I'm in love with Continental Shoemakers."
"Plans and Provisions"
"Annunciation"
"The Accent of a Coming Foot"
"A Pretty Trap"
"Not Jim!"
"Love!"
"The sky falls"

Most who have experienced the play have little difficulty remembering specific moments captured by these images and words. Indeed the mind rushes to make connections between the projections and scenes in the drama. Sometimes, however, readers make associations between legends and images: the photograph of a "swarm of typewriters" reminds us of how Laura acted "After the fiasco." We immediately connect the image of Jim "bearing a silver cup" with this exclamation: "Not Jim!" Should one go beyond the rudimentary and make other connections, say between Amanda's past "as a girl on a porch, greeting callers" and the image projected as she calculates a remedy for Laura—"young man at door with flowers"—that is probably what Williams intended also, for he believed that truth is never simply a matter of correct responses. The device brilliantly serves the purpose of recapturing the impressionistic qualities of the human memory— Tom's and ours.

Memory colors everything in the play with subjective and personal hues. This may explain why he chose a fairly unfamiliar line from a French poem for two of his projections at the beginning of the play: "Ou sont les neiges." It is from "The Ballade of Dead Ladies" by the fifteenth-century French poet, François Villon. The line can be translated, "But where are the snows of years gone by?" Now how does that help us interpret scene 1? It helps very little. (In fact, the legend probaby would help us better understand a play he would complete soon after this one. Among the "dead ladies" Villon lists is one named "Blanche," the name Williams chose for the heroine of *A Streetcar Named Desire*.) If we know that Villon lived at a time of great social transition in his country, that information may help us relate the context of the poem to Williams's play. If we know that Villon's emphasis in this collection of ballads is on death and love, we also can appreciate the quotation. However, to assume that audiences possess such knowledge of the French language and literature is a bit presumptuous. But Williams probably put the legend there because he considered Amanda a type of person whose passing should give us pause. The projections therefore are like forty-four works of art, each focused momentarily on a screen. Some projections make an impact, and others do not. Some appear to mock the events onstage, while others suggest deep pathos. Together, however, they provide a visual framework for the memory Tom shares with the audience. It is the same with music coming at us from three directions—from Laura's Victrola, from the Paradise Dance Hall, and from "the fiddle in the wings."

The allusive qualities of music especially intrigued Williams, as his production notes make clear. Laura's theme "is used to give emotional emphasis to suitable passages." Like the distant calliope of a circus parade, the music works nostalgically as Tom recalls for us his sister's orderly arrangement of glass figures—her circus. It perfectly captures his memory of his sister: "it is the lightest, most delicate music in the world and perhaps the saddest" (production notes, xi). Laura's Victrola provides strains of romantic music such as the waltz "La Golondrina." She is re-creating musically the atmosphere of her mother's cotillion days. The activity also acknowledges her long-gone father who left those records behind as a reminder of his absence. The Paradise Dance Hall provides a musical background for most of the play. "All The World Is Waiting for the Sunrise" gets to the very heart of the play's social meaning. The dance hall band also accompanies Jim and Laura's climactic scene together. It begins with a waltz that filters through the night air into the apartment. Jim's words are couched in music as he asks: "Has anyone ever told you that you were pretty?" Later he says: "Somebody . . . Ought to—kiss you, Laura" (112). At that moment Williams indicates "MUSIC SWELLS TUMULTUOUSLY." Then we learn the truth about Jim, and there is no more music. The next time we hear the band Jim is telling Amanda about his love for a "girl named Betty." Immediately a "tender waltz" bitterly mocks the rise and fall of Laura's and Amanda's hopes, while Jim picks up his hat and prepares to leave.

Wiliams incorporated cinematic techniques in *The Glass Menagerie* as a means to allow the audience to gain access to Tom's memory. Tom remembers an image before he re-creates the dialogue. In his memory the dialogue achieves poetic texture, evoking a touching lyricism. There is a peril here, of course, and Williams was aware of it. To recover the subjective past with such immediacy tempts one to assume that one's personal vision is the only vision that makes sense. The movies, however, taught Williams how to avoid solipsism. Fundamentally the music and projections, especially the projections, function as benign distractions. When directors follow the acting edition of the play and eliminate most of the distractions, they focus more subjectively on the lyrical aspects of Tom's memory. (Thus the play so easily becomes too sentimental, too easily dominated by Amanda.) The forty-four interruptions—"NOT JIM!" "TERROR!" "AH!" "HA!" etc.—force the audience to take a few steps back from the events and to join Tom whose memory as narrator contains the safety devices of distraction. The primary function of the most controversial aspect of Williams's technique is objectivity. But is not this precisely correct for a narrator who speaks most of his lines with an almost annoying sense of detachment? It is the only way he can tell the story without being consumed by guilt and regret.

Memory touches the heart in *The Glass Menagerie,* but it never breaks it. Such is the chief virtue of Williams's sense of distance. Without this sense, Tom might begin the long and difficult mission of the voyager, but he would never complete it. The candles lighting Laura's face are far too strong, far too magnetic. The vision of Amanda comforting Laura is like the music of the sirens of the sea who seek to lure to destruction the first great voyager, Odysseus. Such profound longings can turn an adventurer's face away from destiny. Tom experiences these longings, but, like Odysseus, he has another great purpose: he longs for the truth. Tom's secret is that he has learned to live with the past rather than in it. He accepts his past with neither resignation nor complete understanding. Rather Tom has learned that his mission as a voyager requires him to keep searching for the truth, even if the search constantly brings him back to his past.

In classical tragedy the hero also lives in a world of memory, and he often has difficulty coping with the past. In tragedy that is where the problem always seems to begin—the past. The origin of the suffering of humanity, as portrayed by Oedipus, lies in the unremembered past. Oedipus acts as though he were innocent of wrongdoing.

Tradition and Technique

Through a crushing series of events, he discovers that the source of evil in the kingdom is himself. Faced with the truth, he recognizes it and takes action, blinding himself and thereby cleansing and renewing both himself and the citizens of Thebes. Historical circumstances of Elizabethan England are quite different from those of Athens in the age of Sophocles. Yet Shakespeare's tragedies suggest that the fundamental problem faced by the hero is the past. Hamlet learns that the gnawing problem he faces essentially is moral in nature: the entire kingdom has been corrupted by the king's outrageous sins. The only solution is to expose the source of corruption—a task he eventually accomplishes after much hesitation. Tragic heroes cause suffering, endure suffering, and redeem suffering.

Although he was not using the term in its classical sense, Williams found it helpful to discuss his characters' situations as tragic. In a preface to *The Rose Tattoo,* entitled "The Timeless World of a Play," he writes:

> Yet plays in the tragic tradition offer us a view of certain moral values in violent juxtaposition. Because we do not participate, except as spectators, we can view them clearly, within the limits of our emotional equipment. These people on the stage do not return our looks. We do not have to answer their questions nor make any sign of being in company with them, nor do we have to compete with their virtues nor resist their offenses. All at once, for this reason, we are able to *see them!* Our hearts are wrung by recognition and pity, so that the dusky shell of the auditorium where we are gathered anonymously together is flooded with an almost liquid warmth of unchecked human sympathies, relieved of self-consciousness, allowed to function. . . . So successfully have we disguised from ourselves the intensity of our own feelings, the sensibility of our own hearts, that plays in the tragic tradition have begun to seem untrue.

The fall of the hero of classical tragedy does not take place in Williams's plays nor does it occur in most other modern plays. But his protagonists lead the audience toward a sense of recognition about the deeper meaning of the spectacle onstage. Williams's plays take place in the age of the antihero, when moral values are not so commonly held. Justice, goodness, nobility—these concepts no longer have the same meaning for everyone. Philosophers and social scientists have encouraged us to probe these concepts, and opinions vary about their meaning today. The Greek hero lived with a fixed order. The moral universe he lived in was far less ambiguous than that of his modern counterpart. The antihero lives among a disorder of relativity but nevertheless has a mission.

Tom Wingfield, like many other protagonists in modern literature, is an antihero. He lacks those superior social and/or moral qualifications we associate with heroic figures. The Wingfields do not belong to the ruling class. We see in this lower-middle-class apartment, nevertheless, much suffering. A remarkable achievement of *The Glass Menagerie* is the depth of its exploration of the nature of despair. But the play does not end in despair. Tom chooses to become a voyager, to begin a quest, because he believes that there is a source of meaning beyond the ash pits of modern civilization he encounters in that St. Louis apartment. As he engages in his long journey, he discovers that a key to understanding lies in the past. What can redeem the suffering of modern man? The answer lies in the vision of his sister, comforted by his mother—the illusion that haunts him as he quests for the truth. This illusion brings Tom to the threshold of truth. Magically the illusion both attracts and repels at the same time.

So Tom continues to be pursued, but never to be overtaken, by memory. Since memory is such a compelling force, there are times when one simply must beg the past to let go. The closing pantomime functions as a ritual, which Tom repeats as he travels through time. It always ends the same way, as Laura acknowledges Tom's request and "blows the candles out." The ritual reminds him that he must be faithful not only to his past but also to his future. Like a pivotal scene in a movie, he repeats the sequence again and again. Once the scene ends, Tom again can renew his search.

CHAPTER 9

The Voyage of Tom Williams

In September 1982 a young married couple on vacation in Key Largo, Florida, were drinking coffee in a small café. They observed a man seated alone at an adjoining table and began a conversation with him. Mr. and Mrs. Steven Kunes soon were talking about writers and writing with Tennessee Williams. The author grew expansive and took them into his confidence. The couple learned that Williams was waiting for a bus to take him to his home in Key West. (They did not know that he had slipped away earlier that morning, much to the consternation of his housekeeper.) Soon the two were driving him back to Key West, thoroughly enjoying the conversation.

When the husband mentioned that he was working on a novel, Williams eagerly encouraged him. "Write a play, Steven. . . . Just write a play. I know you can hit the core. I know it like I know a good wine. Don't be flattered when I say this. You can flatter me by using this old machine here to do the job." Then Williams presented him with a vintage Underwood typewriter on which he said he had written *Summer and Smoke* and *Cat on a Hot Tin Roof*. As the couple left him secure in his home, perhaps they were surprised by the playwright's insistence that they should call him "Tom." Six months later they would learn with the rest of the world the news of Williams's death in the room of a small hotel in New York.[1]

The episode in that café just six months before his death illustrates an important aspect of Tennessee Williams's view of himself and his work: at heart he always was Tom. No one who has reviewed even the bare details of his biography can overlook the obvious similarities between the record of his early life and the events described in *The Glass Menagerie*. Williams told his closest friends that Amanda was "an exact replica" of his mother. Laura's real-life model is his sister, Rose, who suffered depression and anxiety until her parents allowed a psychiatrist to treat her by means of a prefrontal lobotomy. As an aspiring young writer, he held a job with a shoe company, and so on. To assemble a list of similarities between his life and *The Glass Menagerie* makes for interesting detective work, of course, but it does little to help us interpret the larger shape of the drama. What does help is to review the nature of his commitment as a writer. As he told the aspiring novelist, the point is "to hit the core." Ultimately we have to deal with what that Underwood typewriter produced—his literary legacy.

When Thomas Lanier Williams was thirteen years old, he began his career as a writer by publishing his first story in the newspaper of his junior high school. It was a ghost story, "A Great Tale Told at Katrina's Party." Readers of subsequent issues would become familiar with his name, for it was attached to a number of poems. From the start the young man who later wrote under the name of "Tennessee" Williams worked under limitations known to everyone who has attempted to write a short story, a poem, or a play. He had to follow procedures insisted upon not only by demanding editors but also by a demanding public. When he finished a work, it had to look like a story, a poem, or a play. The words he put together had to make sense in the context of a story with a beginning and end. And it had to be interesting enough to read or to view onstage. That is but one way Williams learned the rudiments of the literary tradition—in the school called experience. Biographers have discovered that once Williams began writing seriously, he did not stop. The Chronology shows that, upon becoming a teenager, there is scarcely a year in his life in which Williams did not produce or revise poetry, stories, or plays.

He also learned the literary tradition in a more formal way as an undergraduate student at the University of Missouri, Washington University, and the University of Iowa. By the time he began his college education, he had a clear understanding of his life's goal: to write for the theater and thereby to contribute to the larger body of literature. His purpose of attending college was to continue his reading and to improve his skills as a writer. He attended the classes required of English majors. In his view, the curriculum leading to the bachelor's degree was valuable insofar as it introduced him to authors whose works embodied the kind of achievement to which he aspired. In short, his goal in college was not to establish a record of excellence in general but to lay the groundwork for a literary career.

Within a year of receiving his bachelor's degree from the University of Iowa (August 1938), he was within striking distance of his goal. He won a prize of $100 for four plays called *American Blues* and a $1,000 writing fellowship from the Dramatists Guild through the Rockefeller Foundation. He worked on a number of short stories. By the end of 1940 he had experienced his first off-Broadway opening—a mild disaster called *Battle of Angels*. Between 1941 and 1943 he held various part-time jobs as he completed a short story, "Portrait of a Girl in Glass," which he converted into a screenplay, *The Gentleman Caller*. The screenplay would become *The Glass Menagerie*.

This thumbnail sketch of the playwright's early career merely reviews some well-known facts. The most important observation to make is that, from the very start, his writings reflect an evolutionary process. Williams's experience reflects the wisdom of an old adage known to many writers: "Great works are not written. They are rewritten." *The Glass Menagerie* not only went through a metamorphosis from short story to play. It was revised constantly during the rehearsals for the original production.

The official archive of Williams's papers is located at the Humanities Research Center of the University of Texas at Austin. Other manuscripts and materials have been found at the C. Waller Barrett Library at the University of Virginia, Harvard University, and the New York Public Library. Researchers have begun to study early and unpublished portions of several of his major plays, including *The Glass Menagerie*. First came the story "Portrait of a Girl in Glass," written before 1943 and published in *One Arm and Other Stories* (1948). Then came a one-act play in five scenes; this work apparently became the basis for the film proposal, "The Gentleman Caller." In addition to the proposal is a "Provisional Story Treatment." The next development appears to have been a manuscript of 105 pages written on six typewriters and reflecting at least four different revisions in pencil and ink. There is the acting version of the play published by the Dramatists Play Service in 1948 and revised in the 1950s. Of course there is the version of the play Williams preferred, the reading version published by Random House in 1945 and by New Directions in 1949.[2]

We are beginning to learn from these manuscripts that the play underwent a number of changes, many radical, before Williams authorized the publication of his preferred reading version. The study of different versions of literary texts can provide new insights into the meaning of lines, roles of characters, and techniques of staging. We can anticipate discoveries of new information about the play in the future, and some interpretations, including those found in this book, undoubtedly will be reconsidered in the light of textual studies.

In the meantime we have in hand *The Theatre of Tennessee Williams* in seven volumes, and we can also compare *The Glass Menagerie* with his other stories and plays. A particularly rewarding comparison can be made with the early "Portrait of a Girl in Glass" that appears in *One Arm and Other Stories*.[3] The plot of the story is charmingly similar to the play. The three main characters are Tom, Laura, and Mother. The story is told in first person by Tom, "a poet who had a job in a warehouse." The three live on the third floor of an apartment building on Maple Street in Saint Louis. There is no Paradise Dance Hall down the alley, but there is a garage, a Chinese laundry and "a bookie shop disguised as a cigar store" (97).

Laura in the story shows many of the details of the character in the play. She dropped out of "a nearby business college," where she was supposed to have learned typing, and she deceived her mother. Shortly after the mother reveals Laura's deception, we encounter a familiar phrase, "After this fiasco." Laura has a collection of glass, which "she washed and polished with endless care" (100). She also enjoys her 1920 Victrola and "a bunch of records," "souvenirs of our father, a man whom we barely remembered." She likes the fiction of Gene Stratton Porter, especially the novel *Freckles,* and she seems to have a crush on the central character. Unfortunately the character has a girlfriend called "The Angel," but Laura says she "seems to be kind of conceited about her looks." The situation is similar in *The Glass Menagerie,* only the boy is real—Jim—and his girlfriend is Emily Meisenbach (about whom Laura says, "She never struck me, though, as being sincere").

When Laura is twenty-three, Mother asks Tom to bring home one of his "nice young friends . . . down at the warehouse" (104,106). The one he picks is Jim Delaney (Jim D. O'Connor in the play), "a big red-haired Irishman who had the scrubbed and polished look of well-kept chinaware" (107). He is taking a night course in "Radio-engineering." We learn that Tom's nickname at the warehouse is not "Shakespeare" but "Slim." Mother prepares salmon loaf and lemonade. Soon Jim and Laura are "cutting the rug." The dancing stops suddenly when Jim tells her about the girl he is going to marry. Her name is Betty. The characters respond to the news with mild surprise. Mother comments to Tom: "How very peculiar!" But Laura seems untouched. As she goes back to her room, she says: "There's nothing peculiar about it" (111).

This sketch is intended to entice a closer and more thoughtful reading of the story. Not only does the experience help clarify the meaning of events in the drama; it also gives us entry into the mind of the playwright. We notice how he transforms events and modifies phrases. What a pleasure it is to note a subtle description of Laura in the story that reinforces the play's epigraph by Cummings: "I think the petals of her mind had simply closed through fear" (101). In addition the comparison allows us to observe the growth of Williams as a writer. The reader should find the following comparison rewarding.

First is the conclusion to the story. Following that is the conclusion to the play. Both come from a character named Tom:

Conclusion to "Portrait of a Girl in Glass"

Not very long after that I lost my job at the warehouse. I was fired for writing a poem on the lid of a shoe-box. I left Saint Louis and took to moving around. The cities swept about me like dead leaves, leaves that were brightly colored but torn away from the branches. My nature changed. I grew to be firm and sufficient.

In five years' time I had nearly forgotten home. I had to forget it, I couldn't carry it with me. But once in a while, usually in a strange town before I have found companions, the shell of deliberate hardness is broken through. A door comes softly and irresistibly open. I hear the tired old music my unknown father left in the place he abandoned as faithlessly as I. I see the faint and sorrowful radiance of the glass, hundreds of little transparent pieces of it in very delicate colors. I hold my breath, for if my sister's face appears among them—the night is hers! (111–12)

Conclusion to *The Glass Menagerie*

I didn't go to the moon, I went much further—for time is the longest distance between two places—

Not long after that I was fired for writing a poem on the lid of a shoe-box.

I left Saint Louis. I descended the steps of this fire-escape for a last time and followed, from then on, in my father's footsteps, attempting to find in motion what was lost in space—

I traveled around a great deal. The cities swept about me like dead leaves, leaves that were brightly colored but torn away from the branches.

I would have stopped, but I was pursued by something.

It always came upon me unawares, taking me altogether by surprise. Perhaps it was a familiar bit of music. Perhaps it was only a piece of transparent glass—

Perhaps I am walking along a street at night, in some strange city, before I have found companions. I pass the lighted window of a shop where perfume is sold. The window is filled with pieces of colored glass, tiny transparent bottles in delicate colors, like bits of a shattered rainbow.

Then all at once my sister touches my shoulder. I turn around and look into her eyes . . .

Oh, Laura, Laura, I tried to leave you behind me, but I am more faithful than I intended to be!

I reach for a cigarette, I cross the street, I run into the movies or a bar, I buy a drink, I speak to the nearest stranger—anything that can blow your candles out!

(LAURA *bends over the candles.*) —for nowadays the world is lit by lightning!. Blow out your candles, Laura—and so goodbye. . . .

(*She blows the candles out.*)

As Williams incorporated the story into texts that eventually became the play, he kept some of the framework of the original conclusion, but he discarded most of the language. We gain insight into how Williams originally conceived of Tom's mental attitude: "I grew to be firm and sufficient." The few phrases he incorporated are among the more poetic ones. He borrowed only one sentence intact: "The cities swept about me like dead leaves, leaves that were brightly colored but torn away from the branches." Fundamentally the difference between the two narrations is the difference between prose and poetry. Perhaps future textual studies will help us better understand the concluding last nine lines of the play, which are both unique and ambiguous. What we can observe now, however, is that Tom's closing narration in the play reflects a sense of irony missing in the story. It is thoroughly consistent with his ironic approach, which we have observed in his exchanges with Amanda and Jim. The first line of the play's conclusion is "I didn't go to the moon." It is his final retort to Amanda's "go to the moon—you selfish dreamer!" The last line he speaks is one that twists and leads back to him, for Tom knows he never can forget: "Blow out your candles, Laura—and so good bye."

Although he drastically improved the closing lines in the play, both works focus on the relationship between Tom and Laura. Of all the autobiographical elements in the play, this brother-sister relationship surely is the one most subject to inquiry and debate. The playwright's *Memoirs* are revealing though brief on the subject of his kinship and friendship with Rose: "My sister and I had a close relationship, quite unsullied by any carnal knowledge. . . . and yet our love was, and is, the deepest in our lives and was, perhaps, very pertinent to our withdrawal from extrafamilial attachments."[4] Rose was shy and somewhat withdrawn during her childhood, and her long periods of depression especially concerned the mother, Edwina Williams. The doctors who recommended the prefrontal lobotomy did not fully understand the consequences of this new surgical technique. Mr. and Mrs. Williams did not consult others or inform their children of the operation in advance.

When Williams returned from the University of Iowa at the end of the fall term of 1937, he was devastated. There was Rose, existing in a peaceful state and free of anxiety but forever lacking the ability to relate to others. When people asked about her life many years later, she always replied that she was twenty-eight and that her brother Tom was twenty-six. He never concealed his deep affection for Rose, and his works are replete with characters, symbols, and episodes involving roses. (Biographers reveal that Williams sketched and painted roses in profusion, both as a means of distraction and as a deliberate artistic effort.) Even without knowledge of details of the playwright's life, it is clear that the relationship between Tom and Laura is a key element of the drama. Therefore when Tom asks Laura to blow out the candles, what is happening? Is he attempting to cleanse his mind of guilt? of regret? Or is he repeating the ritual as a means of identifying not only with her but with their mother who in the pantomime appears "with dignity and tragic beauty"?

Taking a longer view of *The Glass Menagerie* within the theater of Tennessee Williams, we can find many recurring elements: southern women, modern materialists, and sensitive poets; the love of adventure, the fear of isolation, and the need for understanding. In terms of theme, we can observe that Tom's decision to search for the truth establishes a pattern for a number of protagonists in future plays. The voyager is not always a poet like Tom, but he nevertheless seeks what "has been lost."

In some plays the voyager sails into life's more tempestuous seas and encounters the terrible forces of destruction. Blanche Du Bois, heroine of *A Streetcar Named Desire,* is a seeker like Tom Wingfield; however, she experiences more dramatically the despair of her isolation. At the beginning of the play she arrives at her sister's home, explaining, "I want to be *near* you, got to be *with* somebody. I can't be alone!" Blanche represents the tattered fragments of a dying civilization, the Old South. She possesses tragic dignity in that she holds fast to a vanishing tradition. Ultimately she collapses but not from internal weakness. She is overwhelmed by her sister's insensitive husband, Stanley Kowalski. Stanley, like Jim O'Connor, reflects one of Williams's bleaker visions of the American future. The chief difference between *The Glass Menagerie* and *A Streetcar Named Desire* is that in the latter play the voyager is crushed by an "all American" who lives for himself and has no depth of understanding.

Alma Winemiller, as her first name in Spanish suggests, represents the spirit in Williams's allegorical work, *Summer and Smoke.* Her opposite is John Buchanan, a medical doctor who focuses on the physical. Early in the play Alma discovers that the only way to relate to John is by concentrating on her physical rather than spiritual qualities. Unaware of her changing position, John becomes more spiritual in outlook. Alma's fate is to become a devotee of physical love, while John sublimates fleshly desires for spiritual ones. At the end we have the distinct impression of having witnessed the stage version of a short story of the type O. Henry perfected. Actually the play more nearly resembles "The Virgin and the Gypsy" by D. H. Lawrence. As Williams adapts the story, he seems intent on probing "what was lost," but eventually the quest dissolves in the smoky mists of this allegory.

A father and son jointly assume the role of the voyager in *Cat on a Hot Tin Roof.* The son, Brick Pollit, is a former football star who has become an alcoholic because he cannot cope with life after the big game is over for him. Williams describes him as having "that cool air of detachment that people have who have given up the struggle." The father, Big Daddy, losing a battle with cancer, joins Brick in a moving exploration of life's purpose. Big Daddy focuses on the mendacity of life—the little and the big lies that people accept as they pursue false visions of happiness. The big lie for Brick, Big Daddy explains in the second act, is that alcohol can solve his deeper problem: "A man that drinks is throwing his life away. Don't do it, hold onto your life. There's nothing else to hold onto." Life continues in the Pollit family, but the central players are shallow caricatures motivated by material goods and physical comfort. In this play the journey of the hero ends in deception and death.

The journey is renewed in the spectacle *Camino Real* as the epigraph from Dante's *Inferno* makes clear: "In the middle of the journey of our life, I came to myself in a dark wood where the straight way was lost." The traveler goes by the name of Kilroy, and he seems doomed from the start. His fellow travelers have highly symbolic roles: Cassanova, the eternal lover; Lord Byron, the romantic in quest of an ideal; Marguerite, a sentimental courtesan past her prime; Quixote, an idealist undaunted by sobering reality. Kilroy, the American Everyman, represents independence, sincerity, success, and courage. Kilroy journeys in a land that, Quixote's map tells us, is barren because "the spring of humanity has gone dry in this place." There are ten blocks on this "royal way" (the preferred translation of the play's title). Instead of restoring the human spirit, Kilroy is defeated by street cleaners whose vocabulary does not include the word *honor.* Yet we learn that Kilroy's mission does not end with his death. When medical interns dissect his body, they discover that his heart is made of gold. At the end a resurrected Kilroy, carrying his uncorrupted heart, joins the dreamer Don Quixote. Like a medieval morality playwright, Williams forms characters for the purpose of expressing spiritual points of view. *Camino Real* presents a touching moment of poetry onstage, a highly symbolic moment, perhaps the proper environment for the seeker of truth.

Another morality play, *Suddenly Last Summer,* takes place in four scenes on an unrealistic set whose interior Williams describes as a prehistoric "tropical jungle" whose tree flowers "suggest organs of the body, torn out, still glistening with undried blood." The conflict is between Mrs. Venable, and her niece, Catherine, who has been placed in an insane asylum. Mrs. Venable cannot accept Catherine's account of the death of her son, Sebastian Venable. He had experienced a mysterious, violent death the previous summer during an excursion to various exotic parts of the earth. Mrs. Venable asks a doctor to perform a prefrontal lobotomy upon Catherine as a way to silence Catherine's chilling account. It seems that Sebastian was a seeker of God. But his image of the almighty was that of God as destroyer, like the carnivorous birds that devour the eggs of the giant sea turtles of the Galápagos Islands in the Encantadas. As though conforming to his image of God, Sebastian was a cruel and selfish homosexual who spoke of young men in the following manner: " 'That one's delicious looking, that one is appetizing' or 'that one is not appetizing,' " explains the niece Catherine. Then she tells the truth that Mrs. Venable cannot tolerate: the story of how hordes of hungry children, some of whom had been used sexually by Sebastian, had killed him in a cannibalistic frenzy. The doctor, however, suggests that Catherine may be telling the truth. The one-act play therefore becomes a moral statement about the fate of those whose lives reflect absolutely self-oriented behavior. The basic problem, she maintains, is that Sebastian had turned upside down the human-divine relationship. Catherine, the one who speaks the truth in this case, however, is at the mercy of those who prefer to cultivate illusions of "normalcy." Here we see the repetition of a familiar pattern: the discoverer of truth cannot communicate the discovery.

Some twenty years after he began writing a story about a young man who leaves home on a quest, Williams wrote two works in which the seeker comes home, as it were. The plays are *The Night of the Iguana* (1961) and *The Milk Train Doesn't Stop Here Anymore* (1962). The former work concerns a man named Shannon who, like a captive iguana at the end of a rope, escapes before he is annihilated. The iguana represents not just Shannon but the whole world, which has been made captive by recent war and rumors of war. Shannon is a former Episcopal minister who was defrocked for "fornication and heresy . . . in the same week." Now he leads a "Blake's tour" of "Godforsaken" areas of Latin America for a group of teachers from a "Baptist Female College." A jealous teacher arranges to have him fired, and he faces despair again, only to be rescued by two women—physically by the earthy Maxine and spiritually by the ethereal Hannah. The latter especially helps him to realize that his problem began with his mistaken notion that God is like an "angry, petulant old man." Hannah leads Shannon to see that one cannot live without breaking down the "gates between people." Hannah has as her travelling companion her ninety-seven-year-old grandfather named Nonno. The old man, "a minor league poet with a major league spirit," seems attuned to Shannon's inner turmoil. Through the example of his thoughtful gestures and especially his poetry, Shannon experiences a kind of conversion. Nonno dies shortly after reciting a prayer-poem about how one's "frightened heart" can become the abode of "courage." Shannon learns to endure and decides to remain in Mexico with the widow Maxine. Hannah resumes her travels, having assumed the role of a wandering ambassador of truth.

Themes explored in *The Night of the Iguana* are refined in *The Milk Train Doesn't Stop Here Anymore,* a symbolic treatment of death. The production notes indicate that it is "an allegory . . . a sophisticated fairy tale." Mrs. Goforth is symbolized by a griffin (the mythological eagle-lion-human). A female counterpart to F. Scott Fitzgerald's Jay Gatsby, Mrs. Goforth rose to wealth and power through her physical attributes. Left wealthy in her early twenties by the death of her husband, she plays the stock market and seeks pleasure. Yet she is not comfortable with the people in her social niche. When she tries to discuss "the meaning of life," her friends look at her vacantly. The play's epigraph from W. B. Yeats's "Sailing to Byzantium" is appropriate, for Mrs. Goforth is not at home among the "dying generations" and longs for meaning. Toward that end she takes in a young poet and sculptor named Christopher Flanders who engages her in extended conversations. He tells her that "sooner or later, you need somebody or something to mean God to you." When she dies of tuberculosis near the end of the play, we do not know whether she found that "something." We know, however, that Christopher serves as the incarnation of the "angel of death," whose mission is to help the dying woman overcome her sense of "unreality" and "lostness."

The Voyage of Tom Williams

As we observe the career of the wandering poet in the works of Williams, we see him lose his way in the "dark woods" of the late 1940s and 1950s. There seems to be no way out for Blanche, as she is taken away, or for Alma, as she waits for a passing stranger. Big Daddy and his son face the same truth that Catherine so forcefully encounters in her aunt—that people prefer lies about life rather than the truth about death. In spite of his native idealism, both born and bred in America, Kilroy is destroyed. But the ultimate fate of Williams's hero does not end in "everlasting darkness," to employ Amanda's words. In the later plays we see the glimmering light of hope, the discovery of courage, the affirmation of a kind of faith in "something to mean God." What we do not see, however, is the keen sense of irony that so thoroughly permeates the words and action of Tom in *The Glass Menagerie*. This significant change in the voyager's perspective accounts for many of the difficulties Williams experienced in his later plays.

Gore Vidal once suggested that Williams developed his talent and his themes early in life and then stopped growing as an artist.[5] Many who have studied his later plays would argue that one can agree with this viewpoint without regarding his later works as failures. Let us think of his literary career in terms of a river that is mighty in the mountains where it is formed but meek on the plain before it joins the sea. Yet it is the same river. And at the end Williams is the same voyager who, early in his life, wrote a group of poems called "Blue Mountain Ballads." He included some of them in his collection, *In the Winter of Cities*. One of those lyrical pieces seems to sing the hidden theme of *The Glass Menagerie* and his other works about voyagers who are filled with a longing that cannot be satisfied. The poem moves with the vernacular and rhythm of the musicians and storytellers of the land of his birth and early childhood. It is called "Heavenly Grass":

> My feet took a walk in heavenly grass.
> All day while the sky shone clear as glass.
> My feet took a walk in heavenly grass,
> All night while the lonesome stars rolled past.

Then my feet come down to walk on earth,
And my mother cried when she give me birth.
Now my feet walk far and my feet walk fast,
But they still got an itch for heavenly grass.
But they still got an itch for heavenly grass.[6]

Williams reveals a theme in *The Glass Menagerie* that he pursued in different contexts throughout most of his career. If one wants to locate the brilliant thread of meaning that runs through the plays of Williams, one should trace the path of the voyager. The path begins down the fire escape of an apartment building in St. Louis, and it leads through the deeper recesses of the heart toward those distant horizons of the mind and spirit.

The old man at the roadside café in Key Largo was on his last voyage. He told the young couple to call him "Tom." And so he passed on his typewriter with a charge he assumed would be kept: "Just write a play. I know you can hit the core." Essentially that is the mission of a voyager: to hit the core of truth. Williams asks himself in his *Memoirs*, "What is it like being a writer?" He replies that "It is like being free . . . it means to be a voyager here and there . . . it means the freedom of being" (230). That is what Tom seeks, perhaps what Williams found, ever pursued by those haunting memories of the past.

NOTES

1. Historical Context

1. Alfred Hayes, "In a Coffee Pot," in *Years of Protest,* ed. Jack Salzman (New York: Pegasus, 1967), 15–18. The poem first appeared in *Partisan Review* 1, no. 1 (1934).

2. The Importance of the Work

1. *Chicago Tribune,* 27 December 1944.

2. "The Catastrophe of Success," introduction to *The Glass Menagerie* (New York: New Directions, 1966), xviii.

3. Critical Reception

1. Ashton Stevens, in *Chicago Herald Tribune,* 27 December 1944; Claudia Cassidy, in *Chicago Daily Tribune,* 27 December 1944.

2. George Jean Nathan, in *New York Journal American,* 4 April 1945; *Life,* 30 April 1945; *Time,* 9 April 1945; *Newsweek,* 9 April 1945.

3. Burton Roscoe, in *New York World-Telegram,* 2 April 1945; Ward Morehouse, in *New York Sun,* 2 April 1945; Stark Young, "The Glass Menagerie," *New Republic* 112 (1945):505.

4. John Chapman, in *New York Daily News,* 23 November 1956; Brooks Atkinson, in *New York Times,* 2 December 1956; Walter Kerr, in *New York Herald Tribune,* 5 May 1965; Clive Barnes, in *New York Times,* 19 December 1965.

5. W. Kenneth Holditch, "Surviving with Grace: Tennessee Williams Tomorrow," *Southern Review* 22 (1986):902.

6. Richard Vowles, "Tennessee Williams: The World of His Imagery," *Tulane Drama Review* 3 (1958):51.

7. Harold Bloom, *Tennessee Williams* (New York: Chelsea House, 1987), 2, 3.

8. Arthur Miller, "An Eloquence and Amplitude of Feeling," *TV Guide,* 3 March 1984, 30.

9. Esther Merle Jackson, *The Broken World of Tennessee Williams* (Madison: University of Wisconsin Press, 1966), 42.

10. See Constantine Stavrow, "The Neurotic Heroine in Tennessee Williams," *Literature and Psychology* 5 (1955):26–34; Daniel Dervin, "The Spook in the Rainforest: The Incestuous Nature of Tennessee Williams' Plays," *Psychocultural Review* 3 (1979):153–83.

4. Whose Play Is It?

1. Joseph Wood Krutch, in *Nation,* 14 April 1945; John Mason Brown, in *Saturday Review of Literature,* 14 April 1945.

2. Foster Hirsch, *A Portrait of the Artist: The Plays of Tennessee Williams* (Port Washington, N.Y.: Kennikat Press, 1978), 37.

3. Jeanne M. McGlinn, "Tennessee Williams' Women: Illusion and Reality, Sexuality and Love," in *Tennessee Williams: A Tribute,* ed, Jac Tharpe (Jackson: University Press of Mississippi, 1977), 510–11.

4. Dante Alighieri, *Inferno,* Trans. John Ciardi (New York: New American Library), 28.

5. Frank Durham, "Tennessee Williams, Theatre Poet in Prose," in *The Glass Menagerie: A Collection of Critical Essays,* ed. R. B. Parker (Englewood Cliffs, N.J.: Prentice-Hall, 1983), 129.

6. Young, "Glass Menagerie."

5. The Pleasant Disguise of Illusion: A View of the Characters

1. Joseph Wood Krutch, *American Drama Since 1918* (New York: George Brazillier, 1957), 326.

6. An American Memory

1. Benedict Nightingale, in *New York Times,* 11 December 1983.

2. David Riesman, with Nathan Glazer and Reuel Denney, *The Lonely Crowd* (New Haven: Yale University Press, 1961), 19.

Notes

3. Dale Carnegie, *How to Win Friends and Influence People* (New York: Simon & Schuster, 1936), 13.

8. Tradition and Technique

1. *Punch*, 11 August 1948.

2. *Tennessee Williams's Letters to Donald Windham, 1940–1965*, ed. Donald Windham (Verona: Sandy Campbell, 1976; New York: Holt, Rinehart & Winston, 1977).

9. The Voyage of Tom Williams

1. Quoted in Donald Spoto, *The Kindness of Strangers: The Life of Tennessee Williams* (Boston: Little, Brown, 1985) 361–62.

2. For an excellent review of the textual background of the play, consult Brian Parker, "The Composition of *The Glass Menagerie:* An Argument for Complexity," *Modern Drama 25* (1982):409–22.

3. Tennessee Williams, *One Arm and Other Stories* (New York: New Directions, 1948), 97–112 (hereafter cited parenthetically in the text).

4. Tennessee Williams, *Memoirs* (Garden City, N.Y.: Doubleday, 1975), 119–20.

5. Gore Vidal, quoted by John Simon in "Poet of the Theatre," *New York,* 14 March 1983, 76.

6. "Blue Mountain Ballads," in *In the Winter of Cities* (Norfolk, Conn.: New Directions, 1956), 101.

SELECTED BIBLIOGRAPHY

Primary Works

Collection

The Theatre of Tennessee Williams. New York: New Directions, 1971–81. Seven volumes have appeared to date. Also included are his essays that deal with the plays and his approach to the theater. Tennessee Williams believed that the acting editions of his plays, published by Dramatists Play Service, were not suitable for readers since they reflect last-minute compromises with the director and actors who often requested script changes in the final stages of production. The text used in the preparation of this book is the New Classics edition published by New Directions in 1949, which has been widely available since that date. It is the same edition Random House published in 1945 and New Directions included in volume 1 of *The Theatre of Tennessee Williams.*

Books

"The Summer Belvedere." In *Five Young American Poets.* Edited by James Laughlin. Third Series, New York: New Directions, 1944.

Battle of Angels. New York: New Directions, 1945.

The Glass Menagerie. New York: Random House, 1945; London: Lehmann, 1948; New York: New Directions, 1949.

27 Wagons Full of Cotton and Other One-Act Plays. Norfolk, Conn.: New Directions, 1946; London: Grey Walls Press, 1947. Contains "27 Wagons Full of Cotton," "The Purification," "The Lady of Larkspur Lotion," "The Last of My Solid Gold Watches," "Portrait of a Madonna," "Auto-Da-Fé," "Lord Byron's Love Letter," "The Strangest Kind of Romance," "The Long Goodbye," "Hello from Bertha," "This Property Is Condemned," "Talk to Me Like the Rain and Let Me Listen," and "Something Unspoken."

You Touched Me! with Donald Windham. New York: French, 1947.

A Streetcar Named Desire. New York: New Directions, 1947; London: Lehmann, 1949.

Summer and Smoke. New York: New Directions, 1948; London: Lehmann, 1952.

American Blues: Five Short Plays. New York: Dramatists Play Service, 1948. Contains "Moony's Kid Don't Cry," "The Dark Room," "The Case of the Crushed Petunias," "The Long Stay Cut Short, or The Unsatisfactory Supper," and "Ten Blocks on the Camino Real."

One Arm and Other Stories. New York: New Directions, 1948.

The Roman Spring of Mrs. Stone. New York: New Directions, 1950; London: Lehmann, 1950.

The Rose Tattoo. New York: New Directions, 1951; London: Secker & Warburg, 1951.

I Rise in Flame, Cried the Phoenix. New York: New Directions, 1951.

Camino Real. Norfolk, Conn.: New Directions, 1953; London: Secker & Warburg, 1958.

Hard Candy: A Book of Stories. New York: New Directions, 1954.

Cat on a Hot Tin Roof. New York: New Directions, 1955; London: Secker & Warburg, 1956.

In the Winter of Cities. Norfolk, Conn.: New Directions, 1956.

Baby Doll. New York: New Directions, 1956; London: Secker & Warburg, 1957.

Orpheus Descending. London: Secker & Warburg, 1958; *Orpheus Descending with Battle of Angels.* New York: New Directions, 1958.

Suddenly Last Summer. New York: New Directions, 1958.

Garden District. London: Secker & Warburg, 1959.

Sweet Bird of Youth. New York: New Directions, 1959; London: Secker & Warburg, 1961.

Period of Adjustment. New York: New Directions, 1960; London: Secker & Warburg, 1961.

The Night of the Iguana. New York: New Directions, 1961; London: Secker & Warburg, 1963.

The Milk Train Doesn't Stop Here Anymore. Norfolk, Conn.: New Directions, 1963.

Eccentricities of a Nightingale and Summer and Smoke. New York: New Directions, 1964.

Grand. New York: House of Books, 1964.

The Knightly Quest: A Novella and Four Short Stories. New York: New Directions, 1966.

Kingdom of Earth. New York: New Directions, 1967.

The Two-Character Play. New York: New Directions, 1969.

Dragon Country. New York: New Directions, 1970. Contains "In the Bar of a Tokyo Hotel," "I Rise in Flame, Cried the Phoenix," "The Mutilated," "I Can't Imagine Tomorrow," "Confessional," "The Frosted Glass Coffin," "The Gnadiges Fraulein," and "A Perfect Analysis Given by a Parrot."

Small Craft Warnings. New York: New Directions, 1972; London: Secker & Warburg, 1973.

Out Cry. New York: New Directions, 1973.

Eight Mortal Ladies Possessed. New York: New Directions, 1974.

Moise and the World of Reason. New York: Simon & Schuster, 1975; London: Allen, 1976.

Memoirs. New York: Doubleday, 1975.

Androgyne, Mon Amour. New York: New Directions, 1977.

Where I Live: Selected Essays. New York: New Directions, 1978.

Vieux Carré. New York: New Directions, 1979.

A Lovely Sunday for Creve Coeur. New York: New Directions, 1980.

Clothes for a Summer Hotel: A Ghost Play. New York: Dramatists Play Service, 1981.

Secondary Works

Biographies

Leavitt, Richard F., ed. *The World of Tennessee Williams.* New York: G. P. Putnam's Sons, 1978.

Maxwell, Gilbert. *Tennessee Williams and Friends.* Cleveland: World Publishing Company, 1965.

Spoto, Donald. *The Kindness of Strangers: The Life of Tennessee Williams.* Boston: Little, Brown, 1985.

Steen, Mike. *A Look at Tennessee Williams.* New York: Hawthorn, 1969.

Tischler, Nancy M. *Tennessee Williams: Rebellious Puritan.* New York: Putnam, 1963.

Van Antwerp, Margaret A., and Sally Johns. *Tennessee Williams.* Dictionary of Literary Biography: Documentary Series, volume 4. Detroit: Gale Research Company, 1984.

Selected Bibliography

Williams, Dakin, and Shepherd Mead. *Tennessee Williams: An Intimate Biography*. New York: Arbor House, 1983.

Williams, Edwina D., and Lucy Freeman. *Remember Me to Tom*. New York: Putnam, 1963.

Windham, Donald, ed. *Tennessee Williams' Letters to Donald Windham, 1940–1965*. Verona: Sandy Campbell, 1976; New York: Holt, Rinehart & Winston, 1977.

Bibliographies

Brown, Andreas. "Tennessee Williams by Another Name." *Papers of the Bibliographical Society of America* 57 (1963):377–78. A listing of eleven works Williams published before he adopted the literary name Tennessee.

Gunn, Drewey Wayne. *Tennessee Williams: A Bibliography*. Metuchen, N.J.: Scarecrow Press, 1980. A helpful arrangement of various editions of the plays, poetry, and prose in English and other languages, indicates location of manuscripts, and includes a checklist of criticism.

McCann, John S. *The Critical Reputation of Tennessee Williams: A Reference Guide*. Boston: G. K. Hall, 1983. A highly useful annotated listing of popular and scholarly criticism published largely in the United States from 1939 through 1981.

Presley, Delma E. "Tennessee Williams: 25 Years of Criticism." *Bulletin of Bibliography* 30 (1973):21–29. An international checklist of criticism arranged by general periodical articles and essays, books, individual works, and dissertations, preceded by a brief essay on the critical response to Williams.

Critical Studies: Books

Bloom, Harold, ed. *Tennessee Williams*. New York: Chelsea House, 1987. This volume of selected essays in the Modern Critical Views series is important because the editor is a leading interpreter of modern literature. Bloom's introduction probes the influence of Crane on Williams and considers seriously his "literary" achievement. Several essays deal with *Menagerie*.

Boxill, Roger. *Tennessee Williams*. New York: St. Martin's Press, 1987. This concise review of the plays focuses on dramatic elements. The discussion of *Menagerie* includes valuable analyses of productions.

Donahue, Francis. *The Dramatic World of Tennessee Williams*. New York: Frederick Ungar, 1964. Using many contemporary references to newspapers and magazines, the author presents a biographical approach to *Menagerie* and other plays.

Falk, Signi Lenea. *Tennessee Williams.* Rev. ed. Boston: Twayne, 1978. This volume in Twayne's United States Authors Series treats literary aspects of the playwright, places him among southern writers, and focuses on how the author's psychology manifests itself in heroes and heroines.

Fedder, Norman J. *The Influence of D. H. Lawrence on Tennessee Williams.* The Hague: Mouton, 1966. Shows how many of the themes and plots of Lawrence appear in different contexts in Williams and makes a case for literary influence.

Hirsch, Foster. *A Portrait of the Artist: The Plays of Tennessee Williams.* Port Washington, N.Y.: Kennikat Press, 1978. Reflects the tendency of many critics to focus on the subjects of sexuality in the works of Williams. After reviewing the plays through his perspective, he concludes that Williams, though "forceful and original" is "our national poet of the perverse."

Jackson, Esther Merle. *The Broken World of Tennessee Williams.* Madison: University of Wisconsin Press, 1965. Grounded in a knowledge of the history of the drama and in an understanding of modern philosophy, the author argues that Williams has changed the form of the American drama in a manner duplicated only by O'Neill. Many of her observations are based on her interpretation of *Menagerie.*

Nelson, Benjamin. *Tennessee Williams: The Man and His Work.* New York: Oblensky, 1961. An early introduction to the life and work of Williams, the volume relies heavily on popular criticism and the public response.

Parker, R. B., ed. *The Glass Menagerie: A Collection of Critical Essays.* Englewood Cliffs, N.J.: Prentice-Hall, 1983. The editor begins with a probing analysis of *Menagerie* as a literary work, bringing to bear his knowledge of texts and variants. The essays, reflecting both early and recent critical views, deal with different productions of the play, literary influences, textual studies, and dramaturgy.

Phillips, Gene D. *The Films of Tennessee Williams.* East Brunswick, N.J.: Associated University Press, 1980. The films, including *Menagerie,* and their directors are treated thoroughly, and controversies about them tend to focus attention on the plays' original meaning. The author finds that despite Williams's objection to some film adaptations of his works, the style and vision of the playwright are revealed clearly in this medium.

Stanton, Stephen S., ed. *Tennessee Williams: A Collection of Critical Essays.* Englewood Cliffs, N.J.: Prentice-Hall, 1977. An introduction, written shortly after the publication of the playwright's *Memoirs,* concerns the inner life of the author as revealed in some of his works and themes. Many essays deal with themes in *Menagerie.*

Selected Bibliography

Tharpe, Jac, ed. *Tennessee Williams: A Tribute*. Jackson: University Press of Mississippi, 1977. A major, balanced collection of fifty-two essays written for this book and one that was previously published, all by scholars who have published critical interpretations of the plays.

Weales, Gerard. *Tennessee Williams*. Rev. ed. Minneapolis: University of Minnesota Press, 1974. A good, brief overview of the playwright and his major works.

Critical Studies: Articles

Barnett, Lincoln. "Tennessee Williams." *Life*, 16 February 1948, 113–27. Writing after the success of *Menagerie*, Barnett focuses attention on Williams's themes and new technique.

Barksdale, Richard K. "Social Background in the Plays of Miller and Williams." *College Language Association Journal* 6 (1963):161–69. Rather than probing specific events, the author discusses how Miller and Williams incorporate issues that concern classical dramatists.

Bluefarb, Sam. "The Glass Menagerie: Three Visions of Time." *College English* 24 (1963):513–18. Amanda faces the past, Tom the future, while Laura seems to live in a timeless world. A review of how time and vision relate in the play.

Brandt, George. "Cinematic Structure in the Works of Tennessee Williams." In *American Theatre*. Edited by J. R. Brown and B. Harris, 163–87. London: Edward Arnold, 1967. Considers works that have appeared as movies as well as motion picture techniques Williams used successfully.

Cate, Hollis, and Delma E. Presley. "Beyond Stereotype: Ambiguity in Amanda Wingfield." *Notes on Mississippi Writers* 3 (1971):91–100. After reviewing critics who focus on Amanda's garrulous qualities, the authors give examples of her wisdom, compassion, and ambiguity.

Chesler, S. Alan. "Tennessee Williams: Reassessment and Assessment." In Jac Tharpe, ed. *Tennessee Williams: A Tribute*, 848–80. Jackson: University Press of Mississippi, 1977. After reviewing criticism of major productions, the author concludes that *Menagerie* and *Streetcar* will be regarded as pivotal in the future.

Cluck, Nancy A. "Showing and Telling: Narrators in the Drama of Tennessee Williams." *American Literature* 51 (1979):84–93. Reviews examples of the role of the narrator in *Menagerie* and other works and concludes that their speeches lend an air of fiction.

Cohn, Ruby. "The Garrulous Grotesques of Tennessee Williams." In *Dialogue in American Drama*, 97–129. Bloomington: Indiana University Press,

1971. A careful study of how pathos grows out of dialogue in *Menagerie*. Also contrasts Williams with Miller and O'Neill.

Corrigan, Mary Ann. "Memory, Dream and Myth in the Plays of Tennessee Williams." *Renascence* 28 (1976):155–67. Reviews the problem of time in several works, including *Menagerie*, and shows how Williams uses dramatic techniques to emphasize memory.

Davis, Joseph K. "Landscapes of the Dislocated Mind in Williams' *The Glass Menagerie*." In Jac Tharpe, ed. *Tennessee Williams: A Tribute*, 192–206. Jackson: University Press of Mississippi, 1977. Considers the playwright's "southern" themes and probes Tom's narrative approach. Suggests that Laura is the symbolic center of the work.

Frenz, Horst, and Ulrich Weisstein. "Tennessee Williams and His German Critics." *Symposium* 14 (1960):258–75. Demonstrates that German critics view his work as very important and reviews theological and philosophical approaches to his major plays.

Ganz, Arthur. "The Desperate Morality of Tennessee Williams." *American Scholar* 21 (1962):278–94. Proposes that Williams establishes a dramatic framework for punishing sinners, although some plays reveal his moral confusion.

Gassner, John. "Tennessee Williams, Dramatist of Frustration." *College English* 10 (1948):1–7. Although the career of Williams was just beginning, Gassner suggests he may have the stature of Chekhov, Gorki, and O'Neill.

Heilman, Robert. "Tennessee Williams: Approach to Tragedy." *Southern Review*, (n.s.) 1 (1965):770–90. Identifying the playwright's concern for tragedy in psychological terms, the writer explores how personalities in early plays disintegrate.

Holditch, W. Kenneth. "Surviving with Grace: Tennessee Williams Tomorrow." *Southern Review* 22 (1986):892–903. A helpful review of recent studies and a brief exploration of the reluctance of some critics to treat Williams's work as serious literature.

Jones, Robert Emmet. "Tennessee Williams' Early Heroines." *Modern Drama* 2 (1959):211–19. Advances the thesis that the playwright's heroines are his best creations and proposes that Amanda is not a tragic figure.

Kalem, Ted. "The Angel of the Odd." *Time*, 9 March 1962, 53–60. Featuring Williams on the cover, *Time* devotes a lengthy article to his career and achievements and a brief summary of his life.

Lees, Daniel E. "The Glass Menagerie: A Black Cinderella." *Unisa English Studies* 11 (1973):30–34. Taking seriously Williams's irony, the author makes plausible his theory that *Menagerie* can be read as a deliberate inversion of the famous tale.

Lewis, R. C. "A Playwright Named Tennessee." *New York Times Magazine*, 7 December 1947, 19, 67–70. This brief article shows how the press interpreted the early success of Williams's plays. This piece anticipates future successful plays, while applauding *Menagerie*.

McGlinn, Jeanne M. "Tennessee Williams' Women: Illusion and Reality, Sexuality and Love." In Jac Tharpe, ed. *Tennessee Williams: A Tribute*, 510–24. Jackson: University Press of Mississippi, 1977. Early heroines are torn between reality and illusion, and they contrast with later heroines who seem capable of love. *Menagerie* and *Streetcar* receive careful attention.

Moor, Paul. "A Mississippian Named Tennessee." *Harper's* 197 (July 1948):63–71. The source of many future articles by writers, since it provides biographical material and opinion circulating in the late 1940s.

Napieralski, Edmund A. "Tennessee Williams' The Glass Menagerie: The Dramatic Metaphor." *Southern Quarterly* 16 (1977):1–12. Viewing Amanda as the central figure, the author explores the character as a metaphor transformed into the drama.

Parker, Brian. "The Composition of *The Glass Menagerie:* An Argument for Complexity." *Modern Drama* 25 (1982):409–22. A careful review of antecedents of the play, a thoughtful discussion of autobiographical elements, and a defense of the screen device.

Prenshaw, Peggy W. "The Paradoxical Southern World of Tennessee Williams." In Jac Tharpe, ed. *Tennessee Williams: A Tribute*, 5–29. Jackson: University Press of Mississippi, 1977. Focusing on the views of the world and "southern" literary themes, the essay treats divergent themes such as meaninglessness and biographical materials especially pertinent to the early plays.

Presley, Delma Eugene. "Little Acts of Grace." In Jac Tharpe, ed. *Tennessee Williams: A Tribute*, 571–80. Jackson: University Press of Mississippi, 1977. Briefly treats the theological dimension of the major plays, noting thematic weaknesses in works since *Menagerie* and *Streetcar*.

Scheye, Thomas E. "The Glass Menagerie: 'It's No tragedy, Freckles.' " In Jac Tharpe, ed. *Tennessee Williams: A Tribute*, 207–13. Jackson: University Press of Mississippi, 1977. After reviewing "Portrait of a Girl in Glass," the author focuses on Jim's role in the play and offers a theory about Laura's enigmatic comment in scene 7.

Stavrow, Constantine N. "The Neurotic Heroine in Tennessee Williams." *Literature and Psychology* 5 (1955):26–34. A study of the recurrence of a familiar female personality, beginning with Amanda and Laura and including heroines in later works. The author locates the females' neuroses in the area of the "superego-id balance."

Vowles, Richard B. "Tennessee Williams: The World of His Imagery." *Tulane Drama Review* 3 (1958):51–56. By placing the playwright's work in the perspective of the South and the moral universe, Vowles elevates his status and argues that critics often disregard his plays because of his record of commercial success.

Young, Stark. "The Glass Menagerie." *New Republic* 112 (1945):505. While largely praising Laurette Taylor's performance, Young comments positively on the truth of the southern motifs and language.

INDEX

Index

Index

past, 5, *35–36*, 58–59, 68; and
religion, 4–5; role as ultimate challenge for actress, 15–16; as Scarlett O'Hara figure, 59–60; and
the South, 5, 35–37, 59–60; and
traditional values, 57

WINGFIELD, LAURA, 19–20, 23–24,
34–35, *39–43*, 46–47, 49–51,
53, 56, 59, 61, 63, 69, 74–75, 77,
80, 86, 91; and the glass unicorn,
42–43; and importance of illusions, 41; and isolation, 41–43,
72; music, 40, 55, 81

WINGFIELD, TOM, 1–3, 5–6, 11–13,
19–20, 23–24, 29, 36, 39, 45–
46, *49–55*, 57–58, 63, 65, 77,
86; as antihero, 84; as autonomous character, 57–58; as central
character, 25; character as interpreted by different actors, 54; difference between role as character
and narrator, 27–31, 49; and the
Great Depression, 1–2, 63; and
irony, 97; leaving home, 67–68,
70–74, 84; and magic, 25, 32–34,
39, 50–52, 73; and memory, 1,
25–26, 31, 34, 40, 49, 53, 74,
81–82, 84; and motion pictures,
50, 56, 65, 69; as narrator, 25,
27–32, 39, 44–45, 53, 58, 63, 82,
91; opinion of his father, 52, 70;
and the past, 58, 98; as poet, 29,
50, 58, 71–72; and self-
improvement, 62; as Tennessee
Williams, 11, 86, 92, 98; as voyager, 69, 74, 82, 84, 98

compared with "Portrait of a Girl in
Glass," 88–91
critical reception, 8, 10, *12–20*, 23–
24
Dean, Dizzy, 56
dialogue as poetry, 30
directors, 13, 15, 27, 33, 44, 77–78
epigraph, 71–72, 89
and Expressionism, 9, *76–77*, 80
Famous and Barr's Department
Store, 37

historical context, 3–4, 10, 26, 54,
64–66, 73–74
initial production, 8, 12–13
lighting, 9–10, 13, 33, 54, 77
and magic, 34–35
Malvolio the Magician, 50, 52, 77
and memory, 10, 80
menagerie as object, 1, 19, 23, 29,
33, 40, 81
motion picture version of play
(1987), 30, 44
and music, 3, 9, 33, 77, 81
narrations, 27–31
New York opening, 14
origin as screenplay, 87
Paradise Dance Hall, 3, 65, 71, 73,
81, 88
Preface: "The Catastrophe of Success," 10–11, 65–66
production notes, 6–7, 9–10, 19,
33–34, 76, 78, 81
reading version, 88
and realism, 9, 45, 76–77
relationship to other dramatic tragedies, 82–84
revival (1983), 15, 34
revivals (Broadway), 54–55
Rubicam Business College, 37, 41,
56
screen projections, 10, 19, *33–35*,
45–46, 62, 75, 78–80
set design, 1, 9–10, 32–33, 63, 75–
78
social context, 1–3, 5–6, 10, 25, 34,
54–59, *62–66*, 71, 74
themes of the play; conflict between
self and family, 10–11, 69, 72;
family unit, 5, 10, 53–54; search
for the truth, 11, 34, 92–93, 98;
the voyager, 67, 70–71, 74, 98
use of cinematic techniques, 6–7, 19,
77–78, 81–82
Victrola (record player), 40, 81, 89
Wrigley's gum, 56

influence of other writers, 6, 9, 14,
18
*Milk Train Doesn't Stop Here Any-
more, The*, 95–96

ABOUT THE AUTHOR

Delma E. Presley is professor of English at Georgia Southern College in Statesboro, where he joined the faculty in 1969 after receiving his Ph.D. from Emory University's Graduate Institute of the Liberal Arts. He is the author of a number of articles and a bibliography of international criticism on Williams's plays and has published articles and essays on Eugene O'Neill, William Faulkner, Carson McCullers, and other modern writers. He is coauthor of *Okefinokee Album* (1981), a study of the culture and folkways of the settlers of Georgia's great swamp, and editor of *Dr. Bullie's Notes: Reminiscences of Early Georgia and of Philadelphia and New Haven in the 1800s* (1976).

Presley has held a fellowship from the National Endowment for the Humanities and received the Georgia Governor's Award in the Humanities at the first awards ceremony in 1986. Students have selected him as Professor of the Year for outstanding teaching. He is also currently the director of a teaching museum at Georgia Southern College.